THE CLIP ART BOOK

THE
CLIP ART
BOOK

A Compilation of More Than 5,000 Illustrations and Designs

RESEARCH AND INTRODUCTION BY GERARD QUINN

CRESCENT BOOKS
NEW YORK • AVENEL • NEW JERSEY

First published in 1990 by Studio Editions,
an imprint of Random House UK Ltd.,
20 Vauxhall Bridge Road,
London SW1V 2SA

Design by David Wire

This 1994 edition published by Crescent Books,
distributed by Random House Value Publishing Inc.,
40 Engelhard Avenue, Avenel, New Jersey 07001

Printed and bound in Great Britain

ISBN 0-517-01773-3

8765

Publisher's Note

C · O · N · T · E · N · T · S

The progress of the art of book illustration through the ages discloses a wealth of visual information that reflects a broad range of human experience and activity.

The objective of this new collection of drawings, engravings, woodcuts and etchings is to provide a taste of this visual feast.

Assembled here are more than 5000 different images of every mood and character, from the grotesque to the decorative, from the factual to the fantastic and from the comic to the absurd. Of interest to the designer, illustrator and non-professional alike, this book is your own convenient and exciting archive of ideas from around the world. From mediaeval Japanese woodcuts to American advertising in the twentieth century, representing a wide spectrum of period and style, here is an extensive compilation that is more than a reference work.

Rather than order the work chronologically it was thought more helpful to arrange it into sixteen simple groupings defined by activity or subject. Inside these chapters we have mixed opposing styles and periods to highlight the salient features of each. The book has been designed to make reference enjoyable.

You might want to know, for instance, how artists have pictured all types of people; the genius, the gambler, the troubador and the malefactor. What do people look like relaxing or at play? Working in the factory or in the fields? What tools do they use? How might they dress? And finally what sort of world do they inhabit, from its greatest buildings to its smallest creatures?

Whether you are working on a brief or just looking for the pleasure of it, our aim is that you will be entertained and inspired.

What is illustration? Was it ever anything more than pictures in books?

In one sense all art is illustration, whether of a specific event, seen or imagined, or even of a mood or an idea or a concept. If we think of illustration as an extension of the ideogram we can see that both writing and drawing have their origins in it. Illustration pre-dates the written word. The ideogram was a receptacle of human experience, a means of expediting access to a common meaning. The earliest illustration was still intended, even up until the Renaissance, for those who could not read. Before the evolution of writing illustration was the text. Afterwards it would remain largely in the shadow of it.

Book illustration reflects its age and culture. It can be scientific, instructive, documentary, imaginative and purely decorative. It is a modern concept to differentiate between illustrations in terms of function and quality. In the Renaissance most books, whatever the subject, were illustrated with the same artistry and imagination. The first illustrated book proper appeared during the Renaissance, so it would seem an appropriate point at which to begin a very brief history of illustration.

The Renaissance, which was really a movement of artists and scholars, was characterised by a weakening grip on affairs by the church and the increasing authority of science. The rise of theoretical science grew from a desire to understand and explain the world. It demanded new textbooks with clear, factual information illustrated with scientifically accurate diagrams and figures. In 1543, the year of the publication of Copernican theory, a young lecturer in surgery at the University of Padua published perhaps the greatest textbook in the history of medicine. Vesalius' "De Humani Corporis fabrica libri Septem" embodies the unique relationship between art and learning in Renaissance Europe. Scientifically correct and artistically excellent, it describes each part of the human body, its structure and function in relation to the others.

The "Fabrica", published when the art of printing was not fully one hundred years old, is thought one of its most beautiful products. *(Bottom C.239)*

One year earlier in 1542 the German botanist Fuschius published a florilegium with the title "De Historia Stirpum". Herbals generally were important because of the medicinal properties of plants. But apart from the individual and exceptional efforts of artists like Dürer and Da Vinci, botanical illustration had hitherto been limited. Usually is was confined to a schematic representation of a single vertical stem with two or three stylised leaf shapes on either side. Weiditz, in Brufel's herbal of 1530, was the first to draw recognizable species, but the most beautiful of the herbals in English is Johnson's 1633 edition of "Gerard's Herbal". The borders of the page are used as a framework to support a rigorous internal logic and coherence of design and the drawings, which never foresake their naturalism, are exceptionally bold and beautiful. *(Bottom R.278)*

Good examples of animals well drawn during the Renaissance can be found in "Icones Animalum" printed in Zurich in 1554 by Conrad Gesner. *(Bottom R.313)*

Although the historical data are scanty we know that the art of wood engraving began in China as early as the sixth century and spread thence to Korea and later Japan. In the early seventeenth century there appeared in Japan a school of genre painting called the Ukiyo-e. One artist from this school, Moronobu, was the first Japanese to make extensive use of the woodcut when he innovated the Yehon or picture book.

Woodcutting conceives the image in linear terms in much the same way that drawing defines the image in black on a white ground. The effect of space relies on the width of the black lines which in woodcut are all of an equal density. Simply put, the wider the line the nearer it looks and vice versa. In woodcut there could be no half tones to create the illusion of distance.

INTRODUCTION

In the late eighteenth century in England the woodcut was alive and well and enjoying something of a revival at the hands of Thomas Bewick who had pulled it from obscurity. We are fortunate that he adapted it to the needs of mass production at exactly the right time to match developments in printing during the Industrial Revolution. The instigator of an English school of illustration and a forerunner of the Romantic movement, of Blake *(Centre L.214),* Palmer and Calvert, Bewick's influence however was technical rather than artistic. He innovated a technique of woodcut properly called wood-engraving. Woodcuts were gouged out of the plank side of a piece of wood, Bewick used the harder end-grain. His images were worked out of a black ground in half-tone and white, giving his figures a painterly three dimensional quality and a solidity that was quite new.

Bewick has been critized for failing to pay attention to the composition of the page as a whole. But whatever he may have lacked in design he made up for in fresh unclouded intimacy of his observations from the natural world.

In contrast to Bewick's deeply poetic approach to nature stands the work of the French caricaturist J.J. Grandville. There is a European tradition of expressing fantasy through the graphic media which "The Public and Private Life of Animals", 1842 exemplifies. Grandville is at his disturbing best when drawing the menacing forms of beetles and other insects engaged in specifically human activities. His greater relevance to art historians lies beyond the artistic merit of his work and his influence on contemporaries Tenniel and Lear, *(266).* He is acknowledged to be precursor to the Symbolist and Surrealist movements.

The nineteenth century if inconsistent in standards of craftsmanship was one of the richest, most formative periods for illustration. A growth in literacy and a surge in the size of the population generated an increasing demand for illustrated books of all kinds which the new mechanical presses were able to supply. Because a wide readership was assured editions no longer had to be limited, and the result was more and more popular editions aimed at the new book buying public.

The new social order stimulated the minds of artists and writers, but not always to generosity. George Cruickshank, a committed fighter for social reform, attacked with a fierce humour the injustices and cruelty of the industrial age. In the same satirical tradition as Hogarth and Rowlandson, Cruickshank elected to use etching as his medium. It was ideally suited to his fluid descriptive line and the distortions and exaggerations of caricature. His most successful work and the best known, are the illustrations for Dickens' novels. The medium and the subject matter of the dark spaces in gloomy gas-lit Victorian London are in complete harmony.

Contemporary with Cruickshank were John Leech and Charles Keene, both humorists who worked in gentler, less spleenful vein. Drawing for the satirical journal "Punch" they burlesqued the manners and customs of the new middle classes, laughing at their attempts to cope with an accident fraught modern age, *(Bottom R. 164, Bottom L. 102).*

The mood of nineteenth century "fin de siècle" will always be associated with the decadent and grotesque designs of Aubrey Beardsley. His eclectic mix of Japanic style and mediaeval decoration combine in illustrations of exceptional beauty. The intricacy of his drawings was impossible for wood engraving, but his mastery of the line block method brought the sparkling greys of his ornately patterned costumes to perfection, *(Top R. 161).*

The closing years of the century saw a growing distrust of the machine in the eyes of at least one artist. William Morris was prompted to revive the craft of the illustrated book at the Kelmscott Press. Although Morris published some notable editions he was fighting against the tide, *(Top R. 235).* The challenges of the new century had to be met, the increasing pre-eminence of photography, the growing absorption of design and illustration by advertising which would inspire the art movements of the 1960s, and possibilities in even greater mass production. Whatever doubts Morris had about the new age, however, we can still concur with his statement that "the illustrated book is not perhaps absolutely necessary to man's life, but it gives us such endless pleasure … that it must remain one of the very worthiest things towards the production of which reasonable man should strive."

No. 100.—Dr. Gall.

No. 101.—Hewlett, Actor.

PEOPLE

13

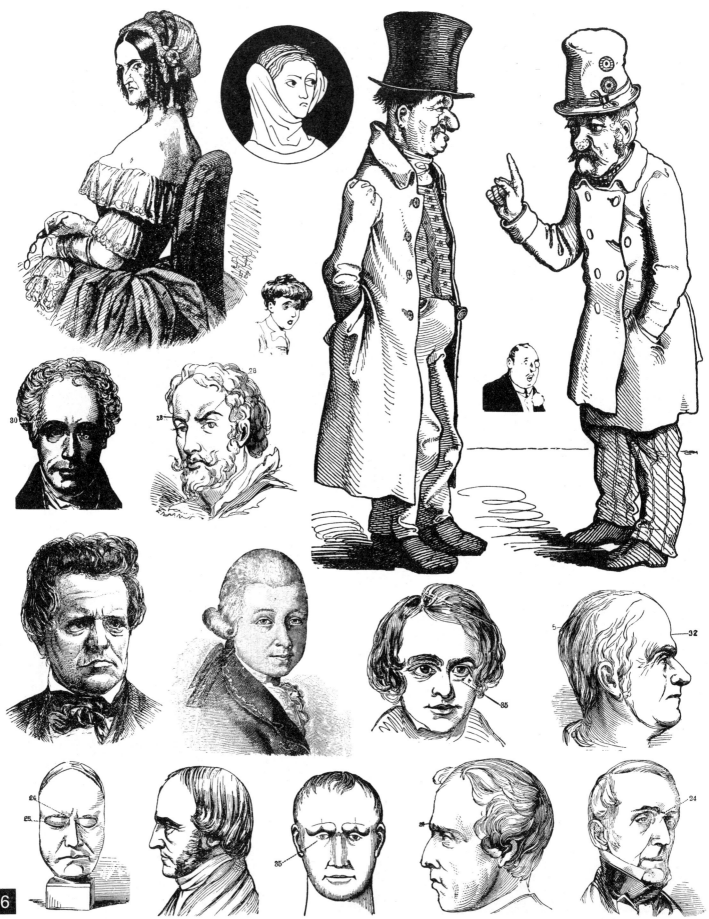

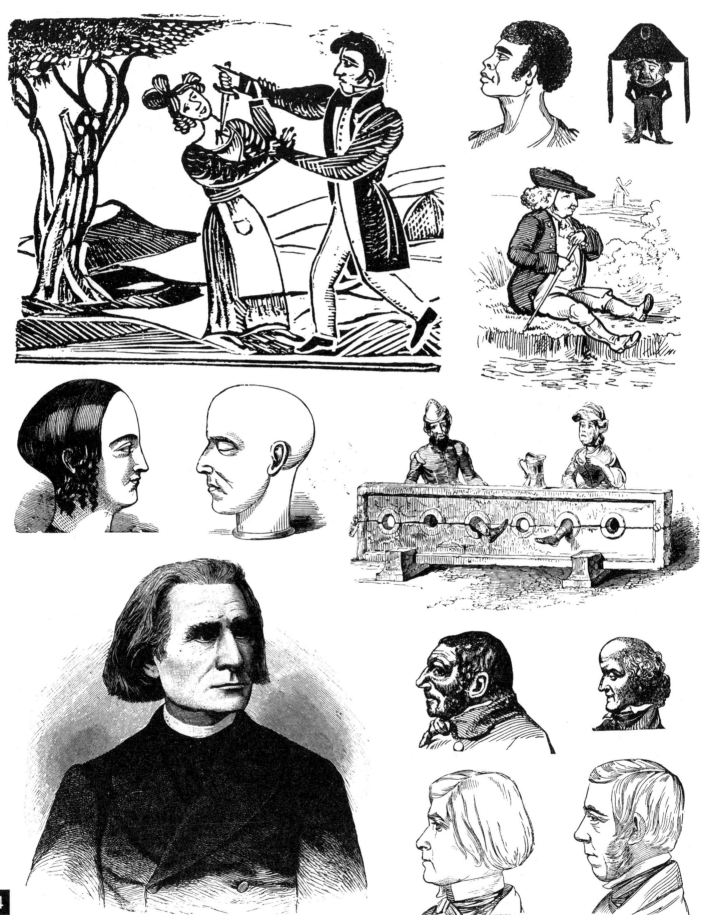

PEOPLE

25

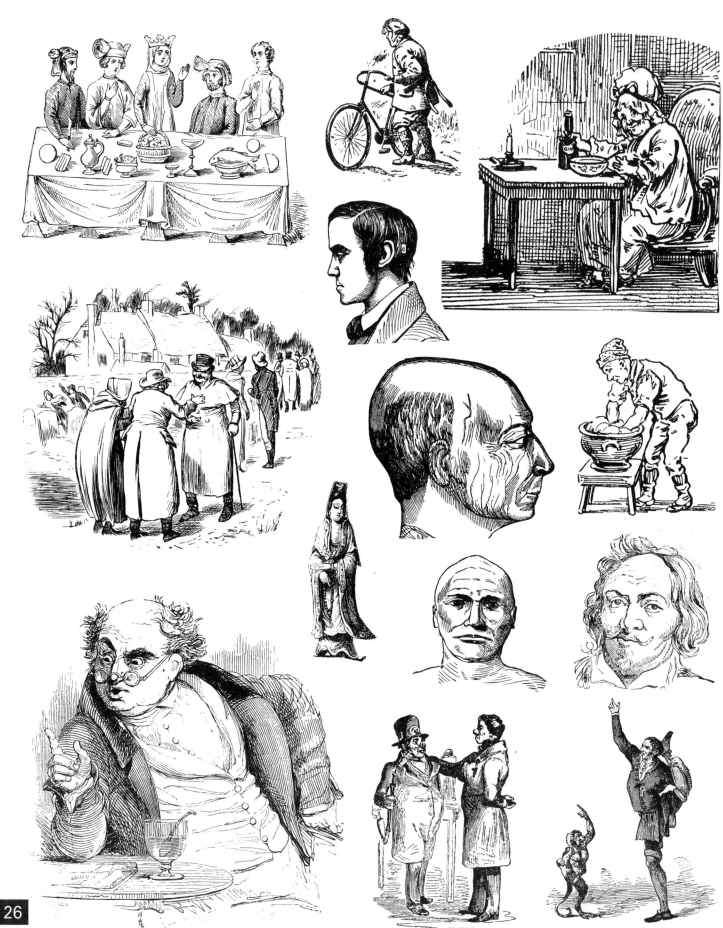

1846. 1847 1848 1849.

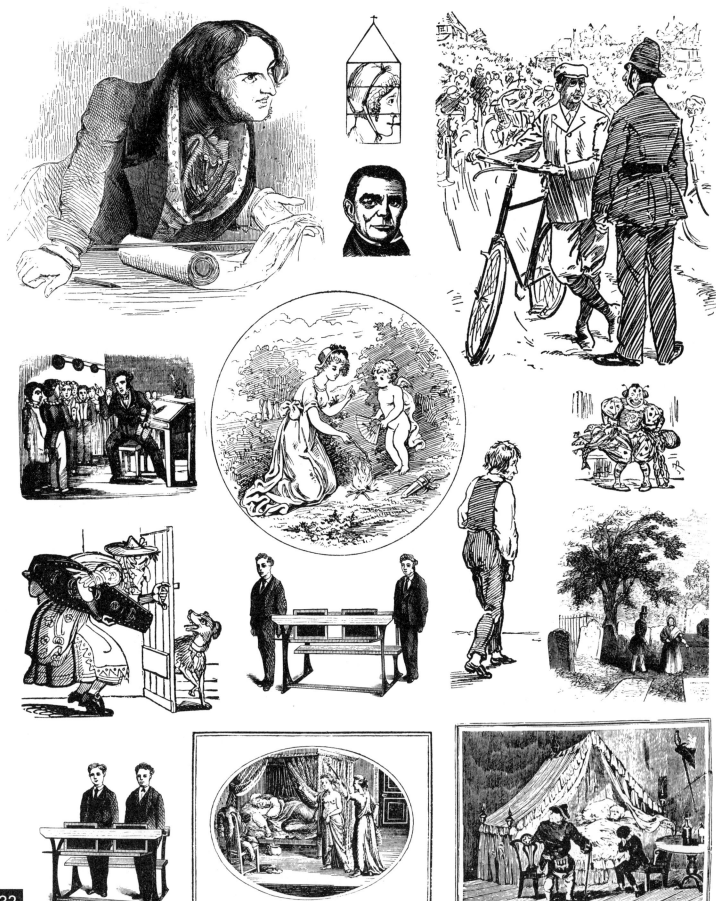

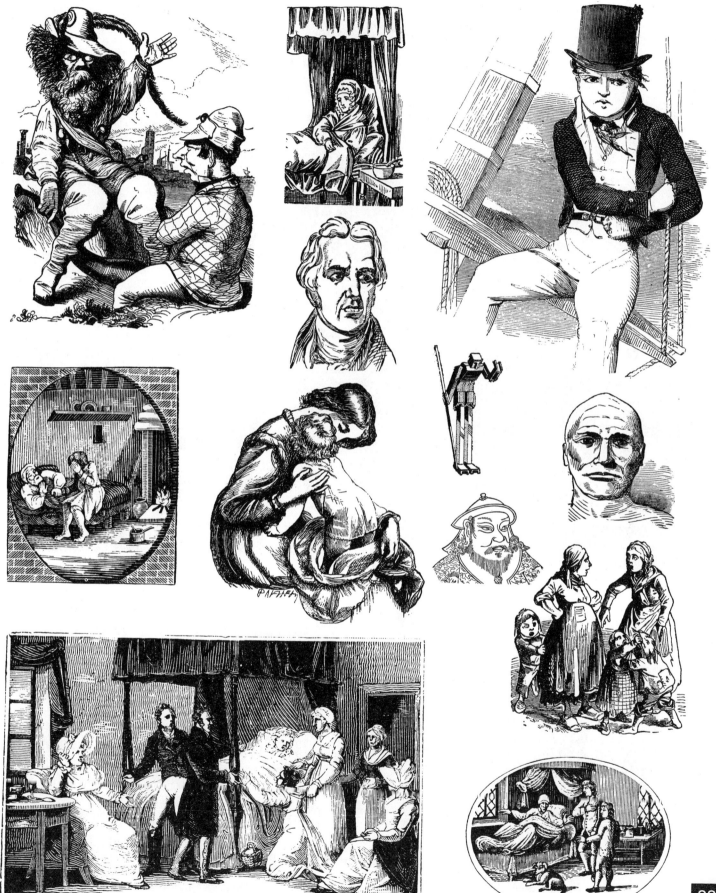

IRON AND SON,
SHOES FOR MEN
AND BEASTS.

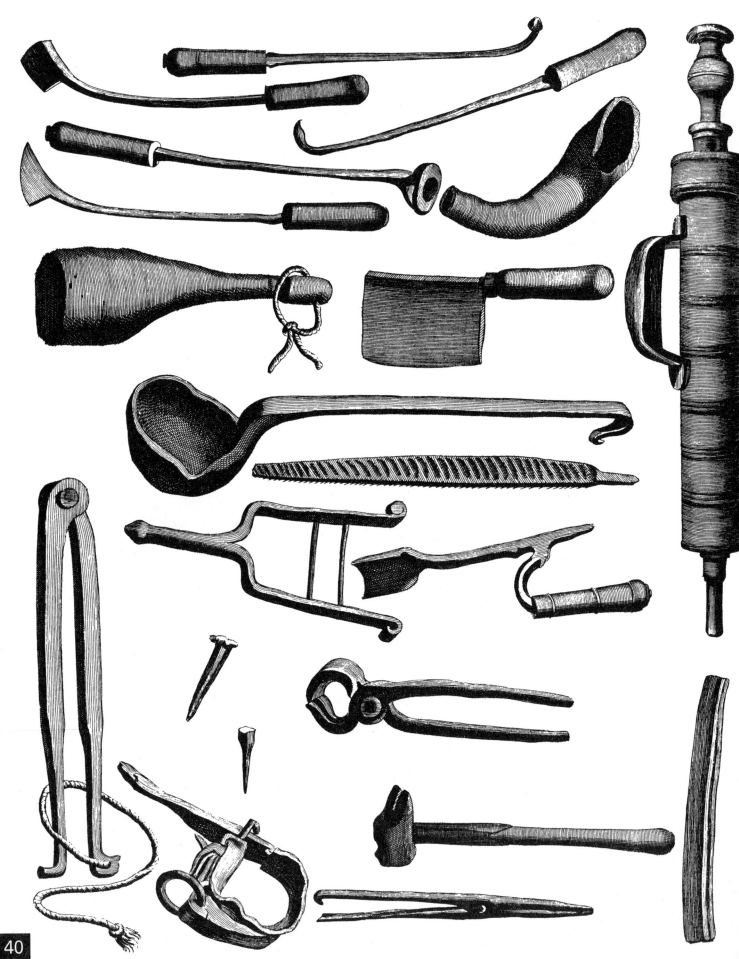

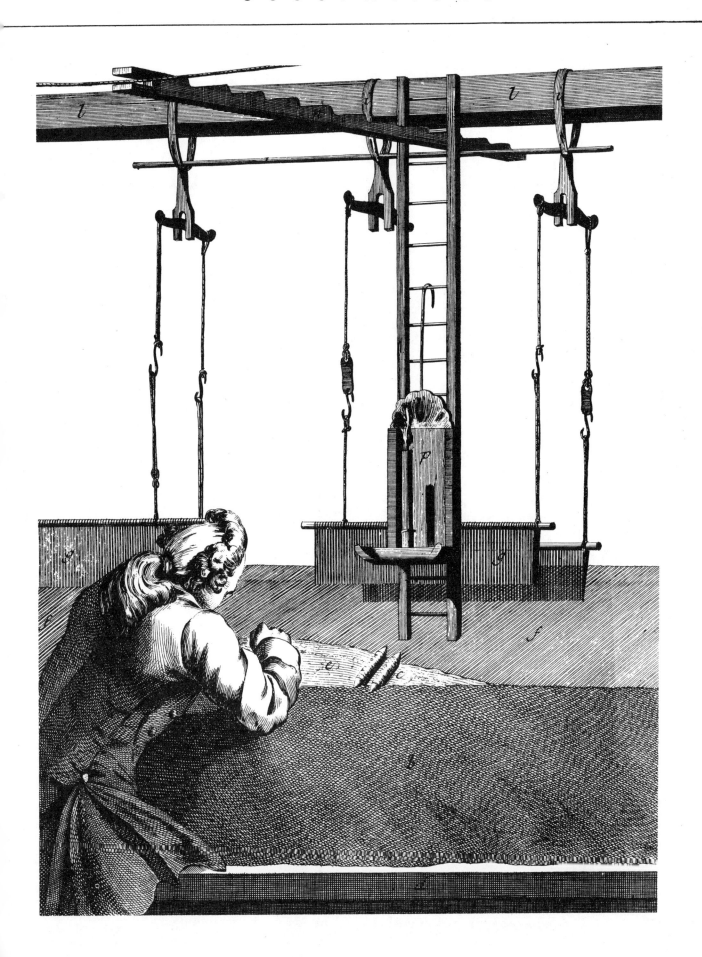

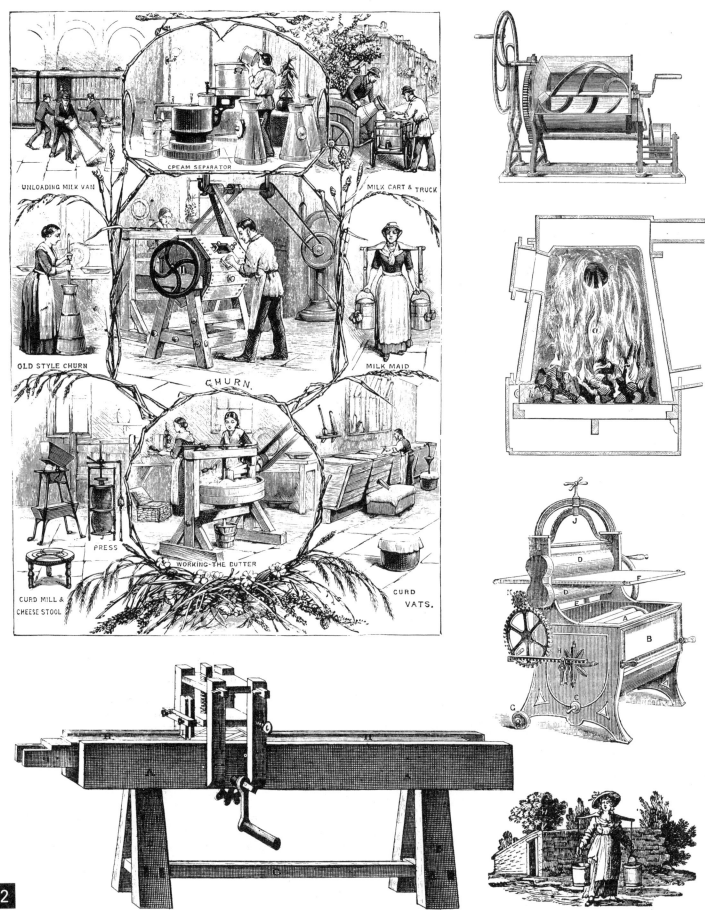

UNLOADING MILK VAN

CREAM SEPARATOR

MILK CART & TRUCK

OLD STYLE CHURN

CHURN.

MILK MAID

PRESS

WORKING-THE BUTTER

CURD MILL &
CHEESE STOOL

CURD
VATS.

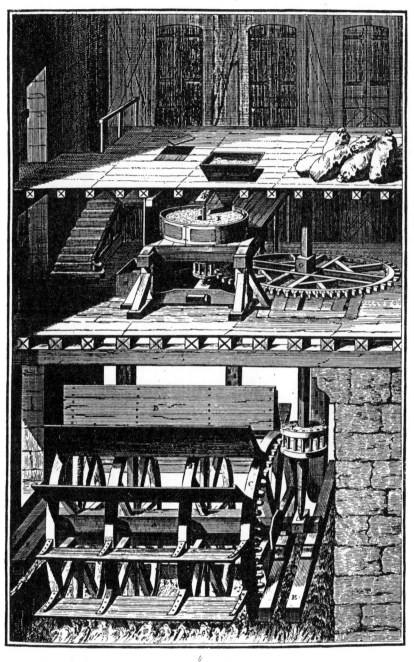

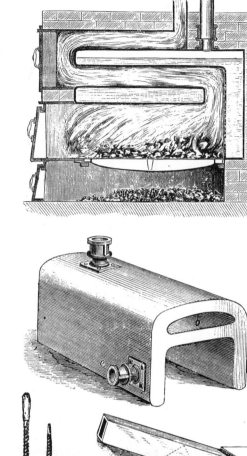

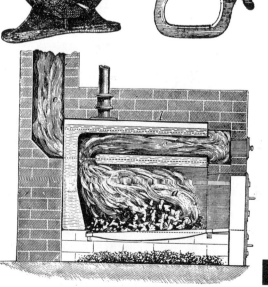

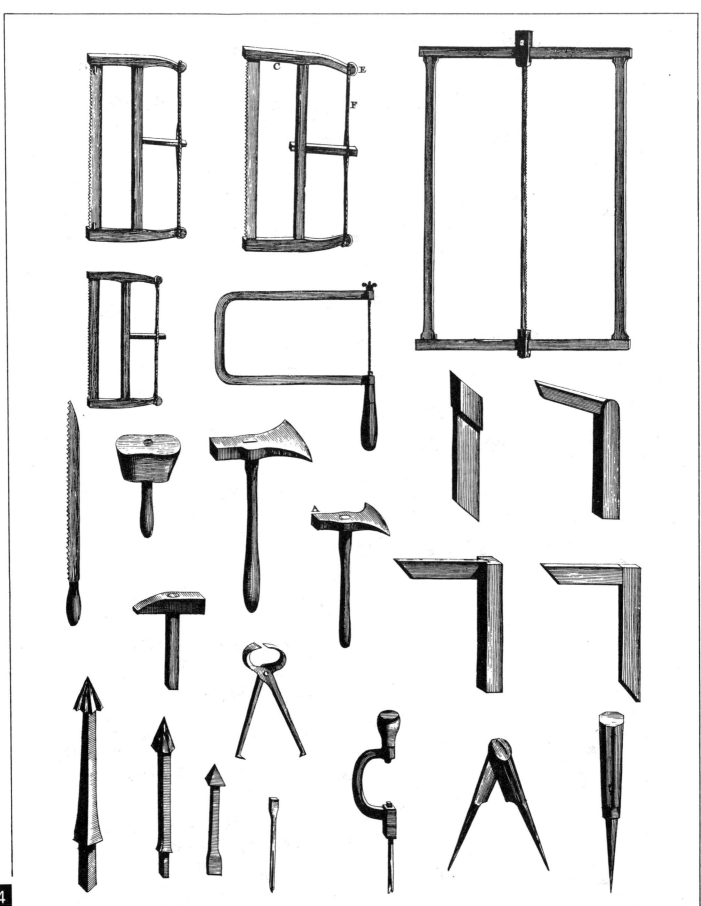

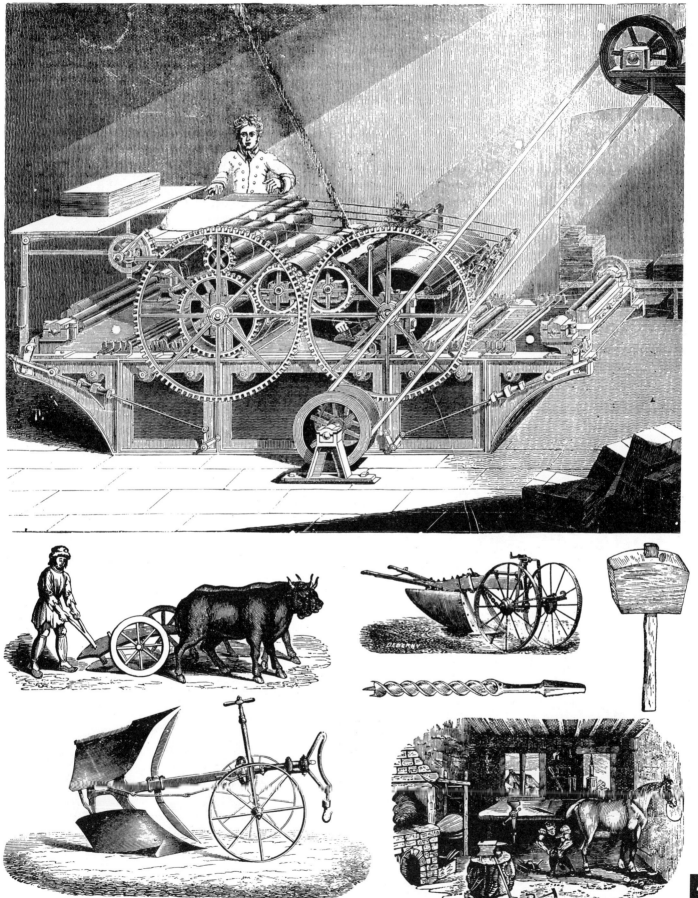

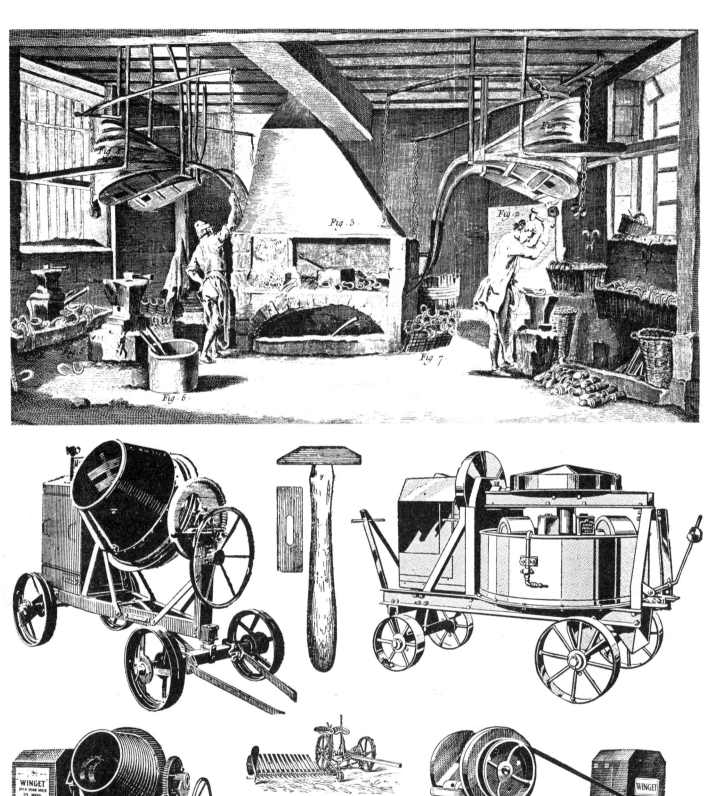

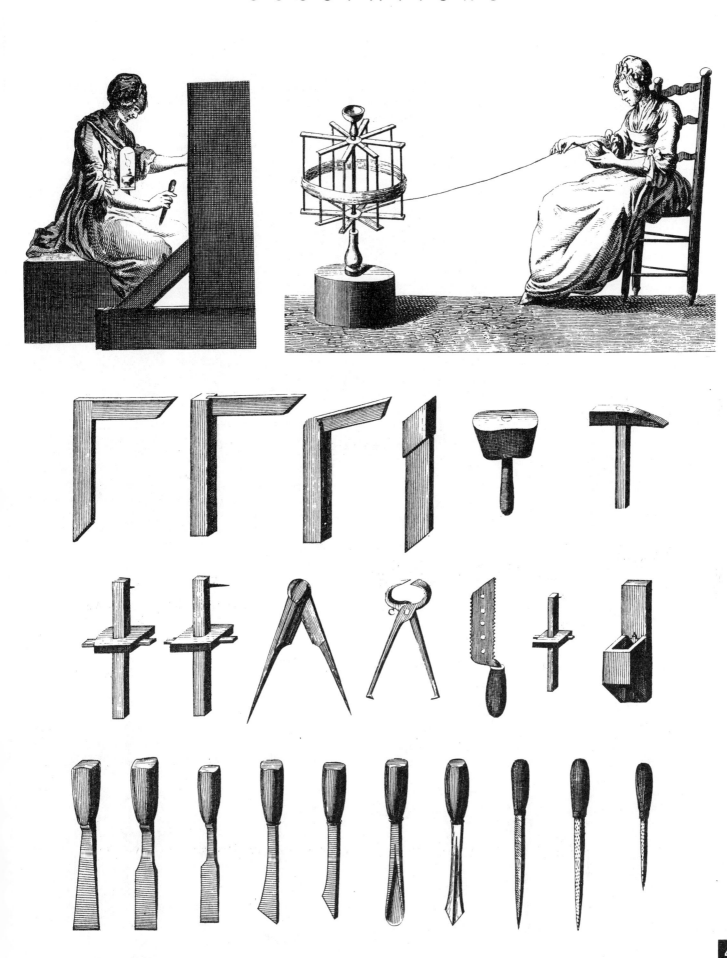

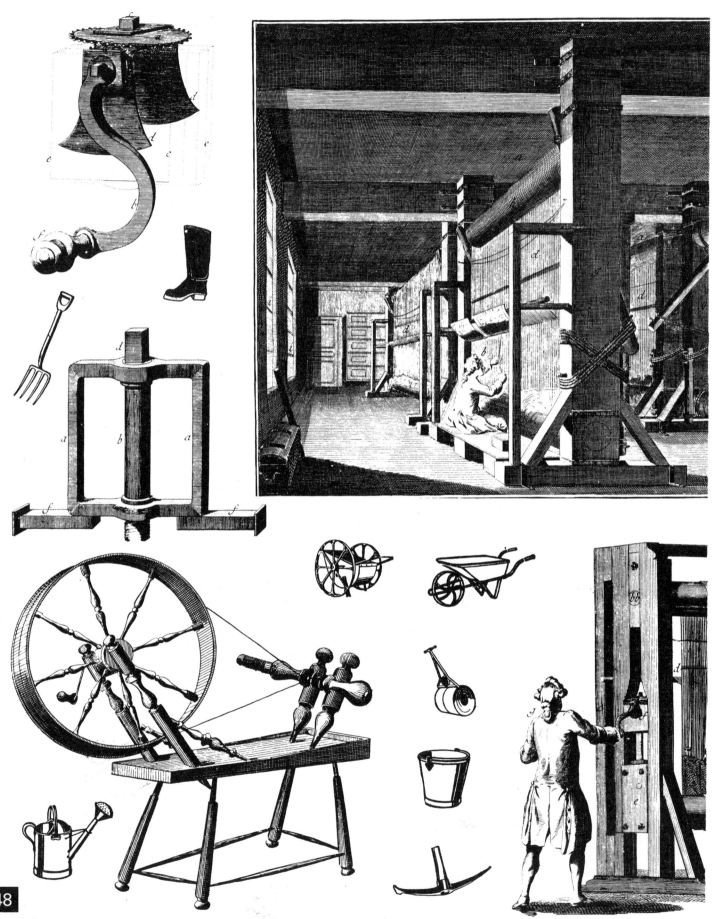

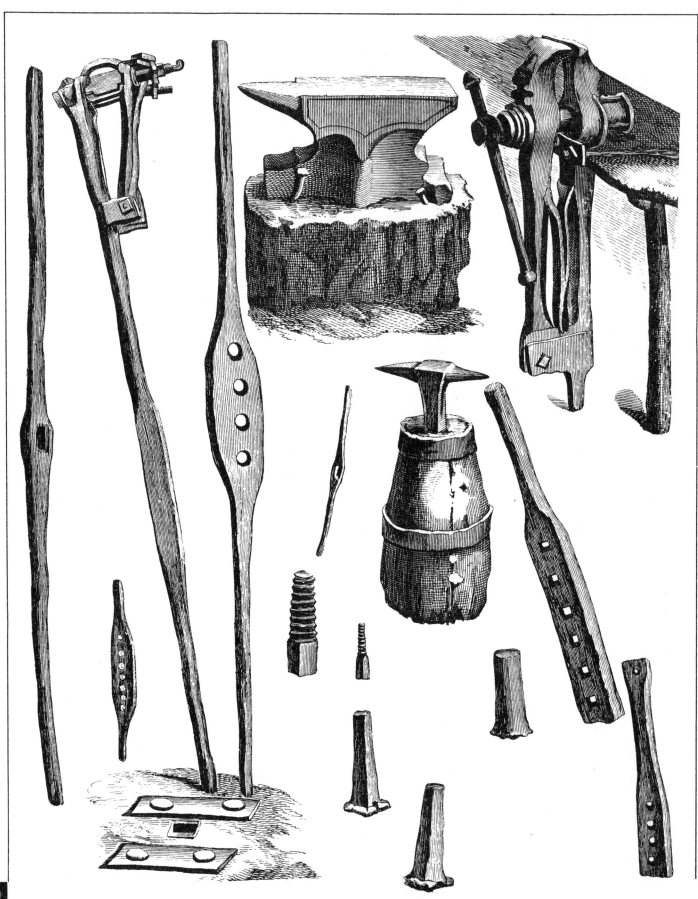

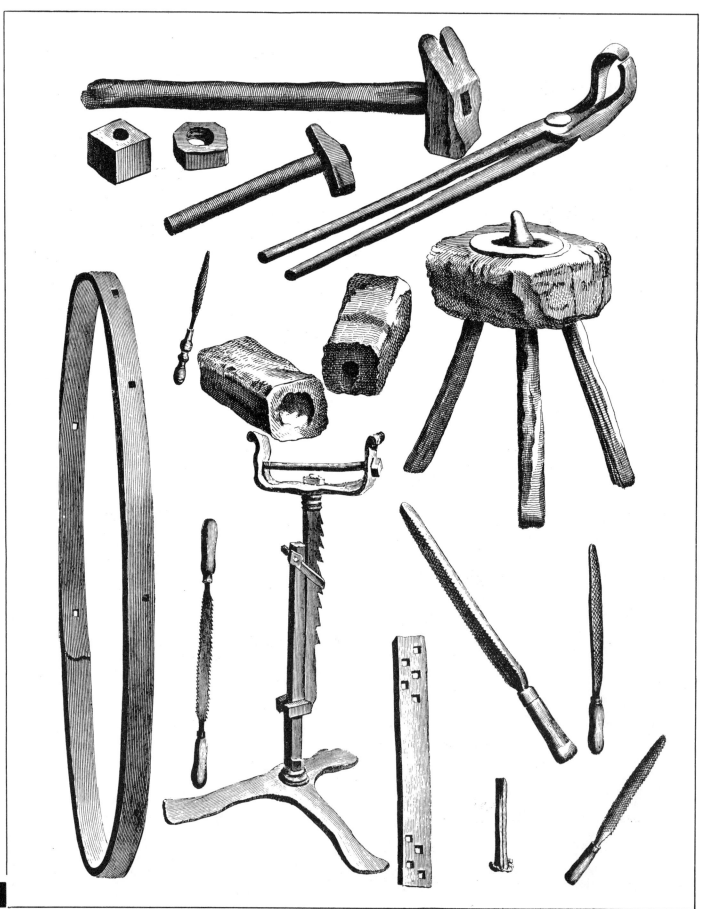

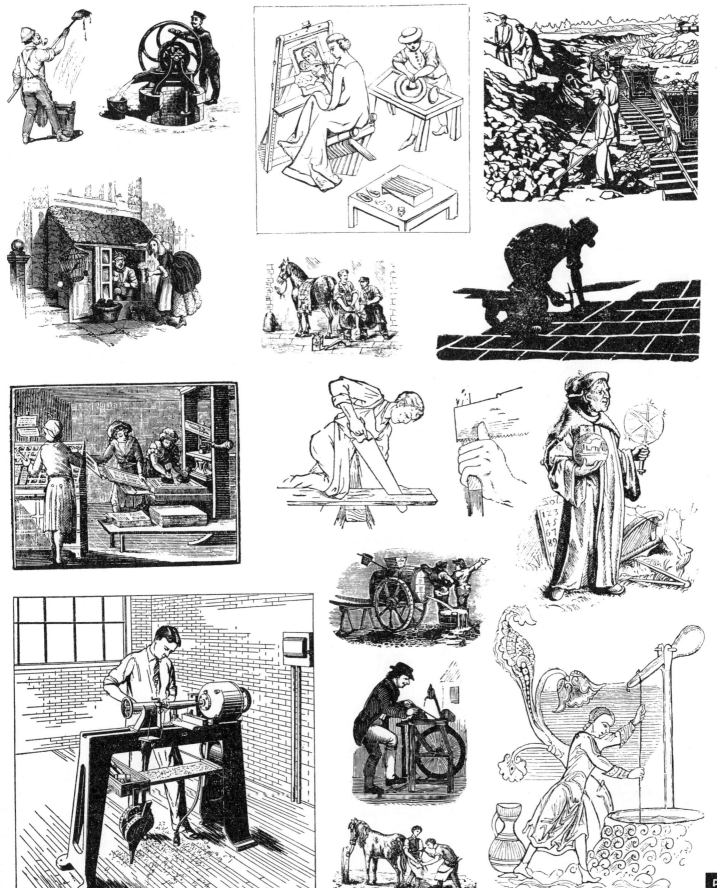

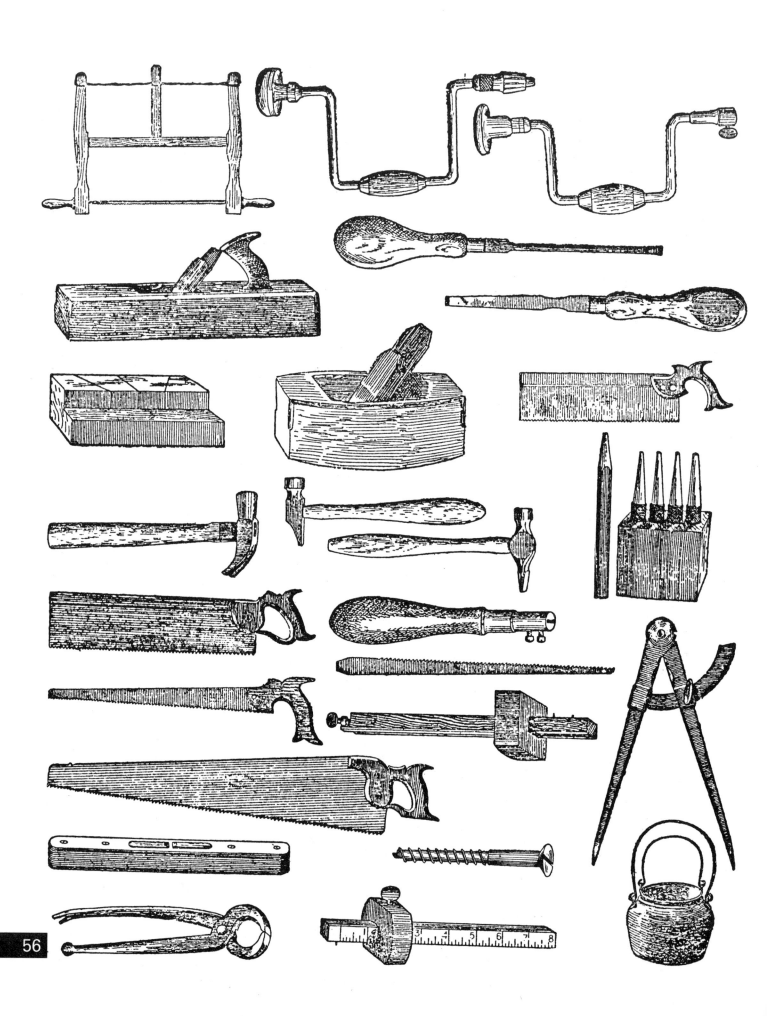

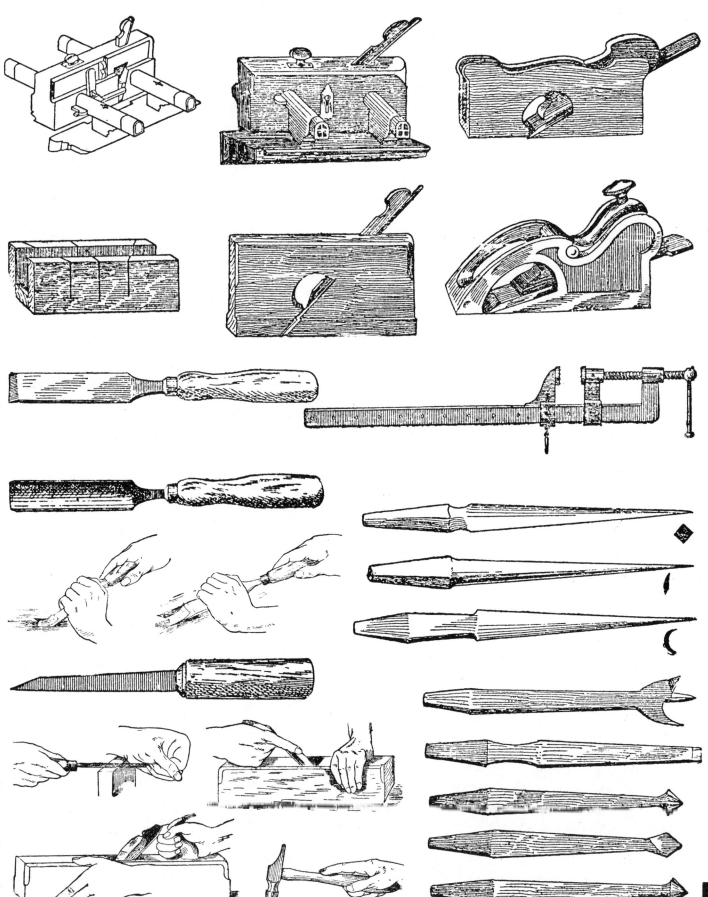

57

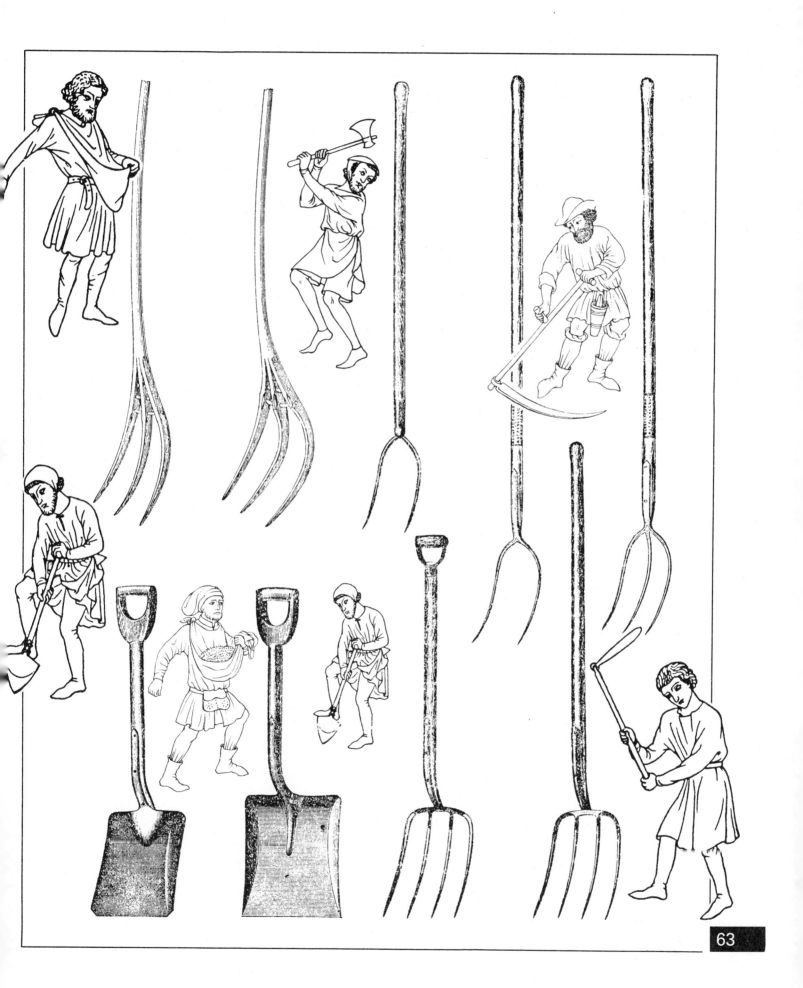

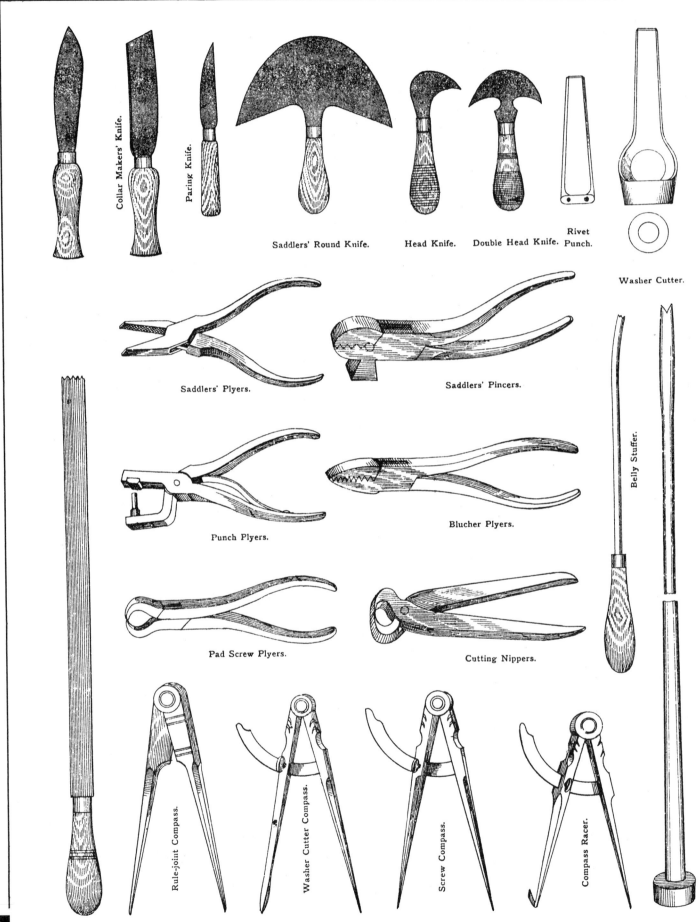

Collar Makers' Knife.

Paring Knife.

Saddlers' Round Knife.

Head Knife.

Double Head Knife.

Rivet Punch.

Washer Cutter.

Saddlers' Plyers.

Saddlers' Pincers.

Punch Plyers.

Blucher Plyers.

Belly Stuffer.

Pad Screw Plyers.

Cutting Nippers.

Rule-joint Compass.

Washer Cutter Compass.

Screw Compass.

Compass Racer.

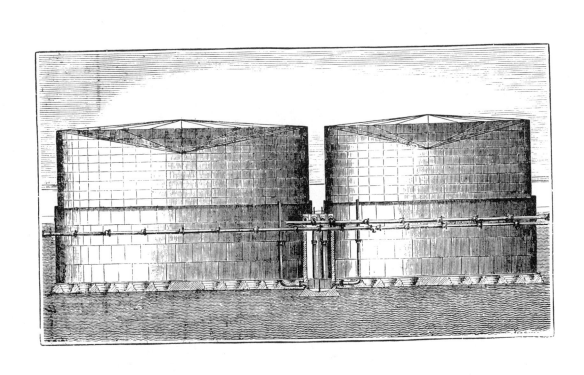

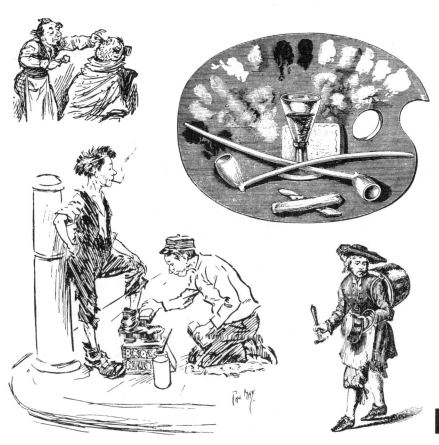

THE PASSING OF THE HORSE

NO FURTHER USE FOR HIM.

SEE OUR STAND AT THE SHOW

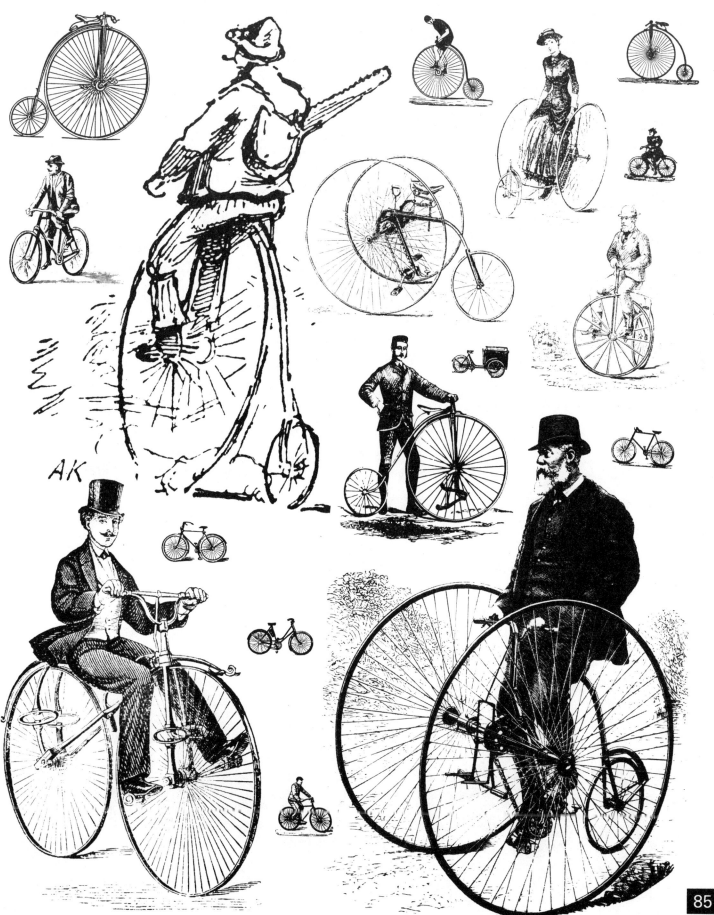

Poop.

Talar

Wale.

Prow.

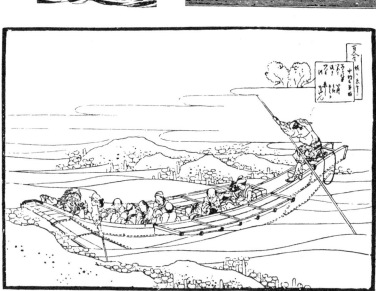

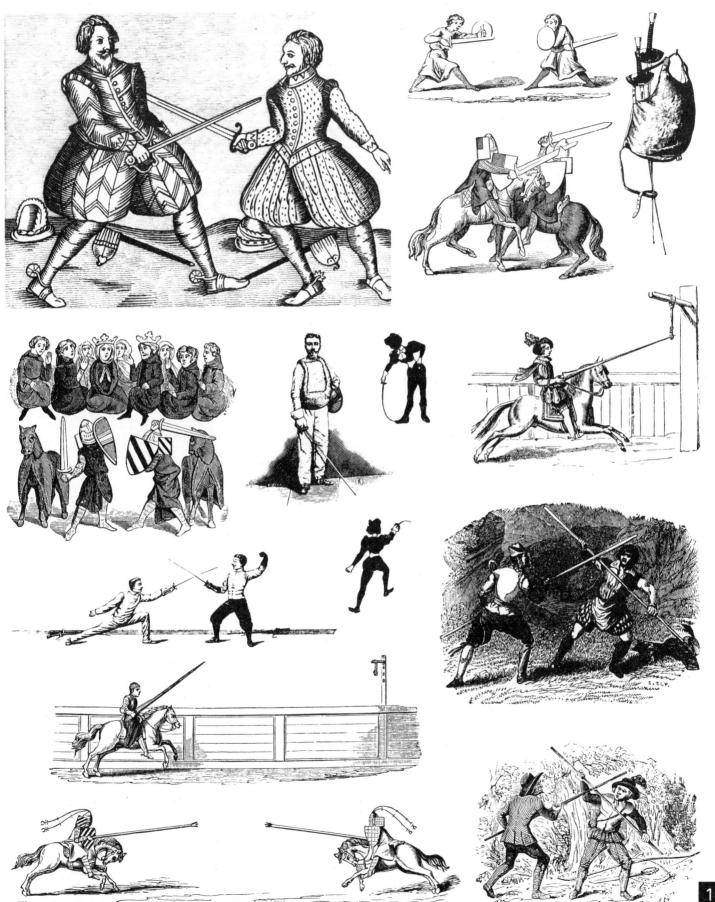

Fig. 2.

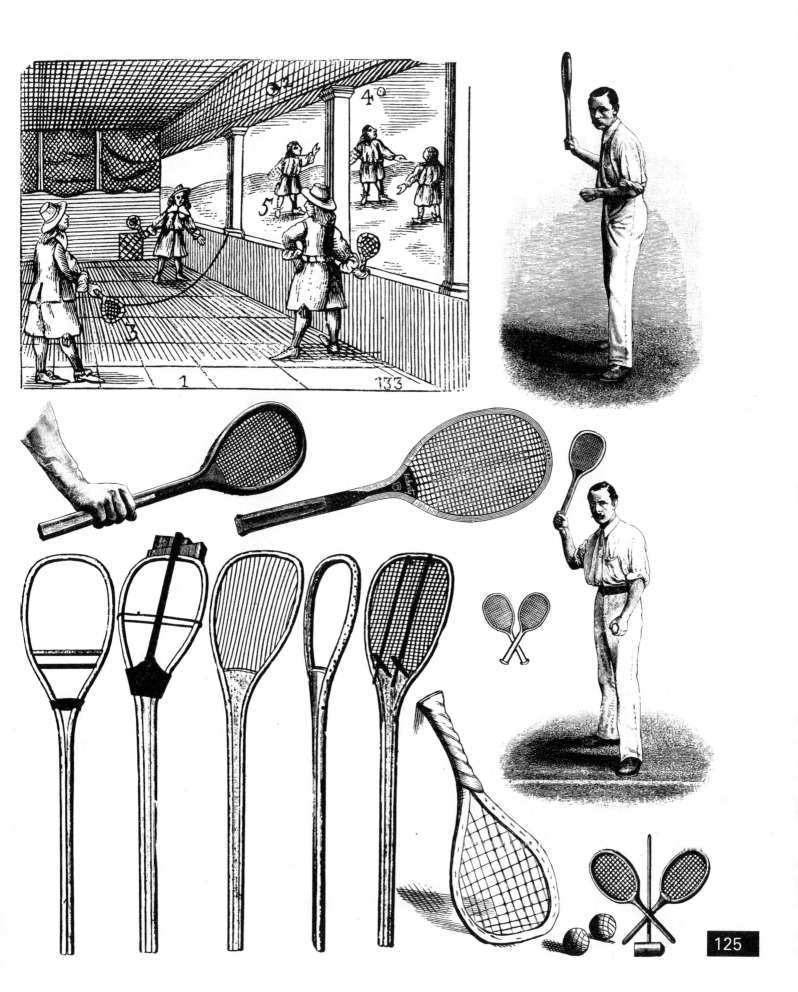

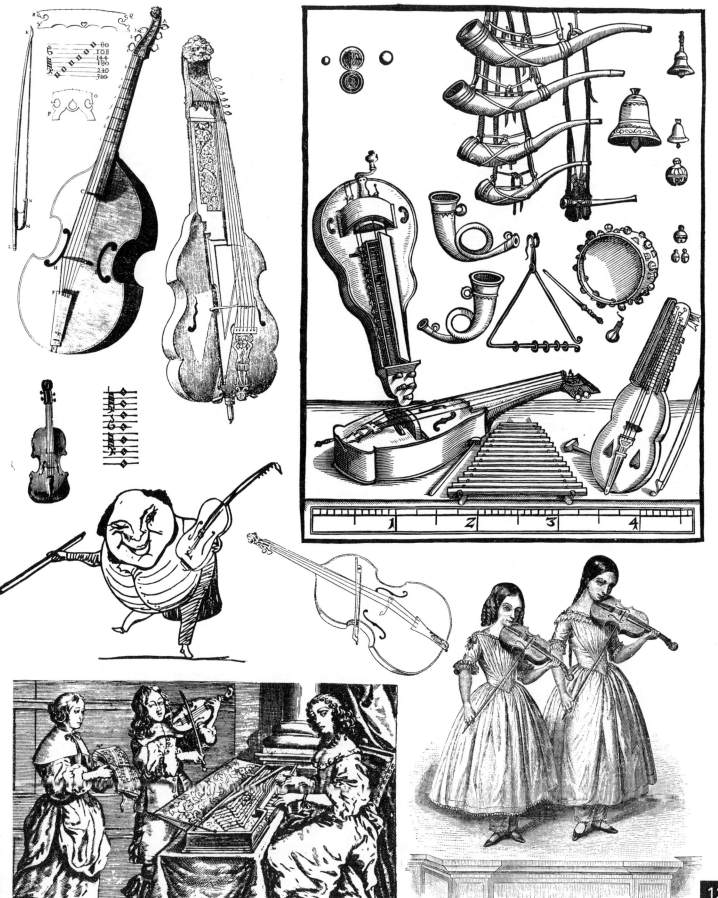

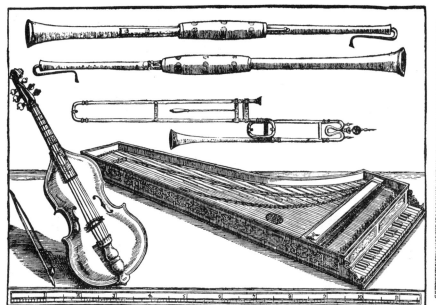

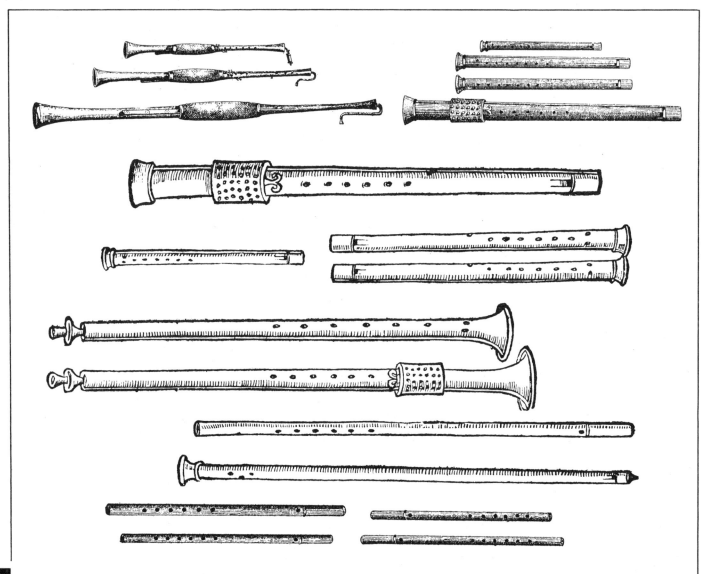

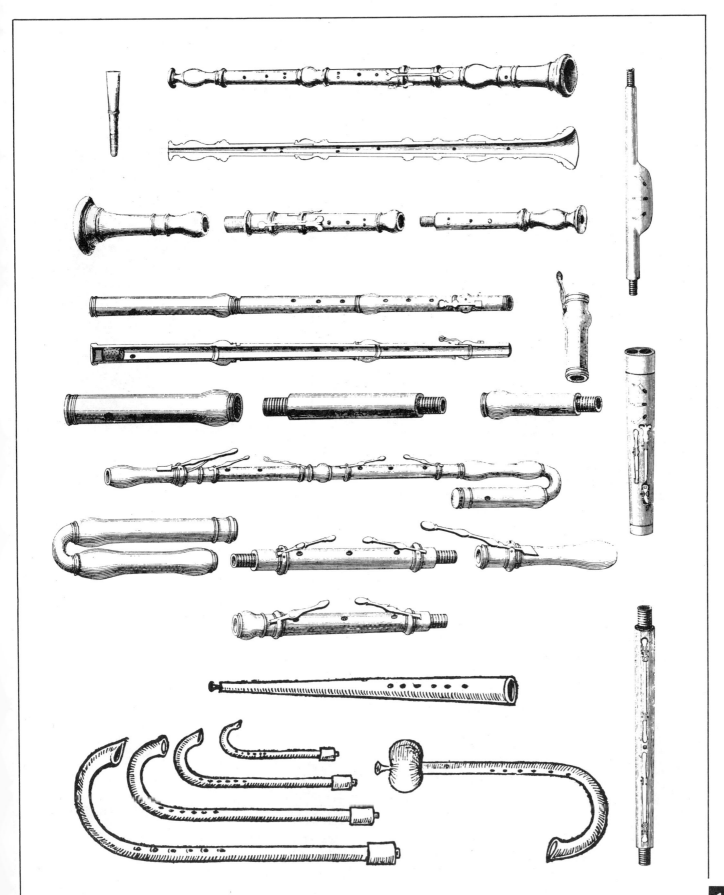

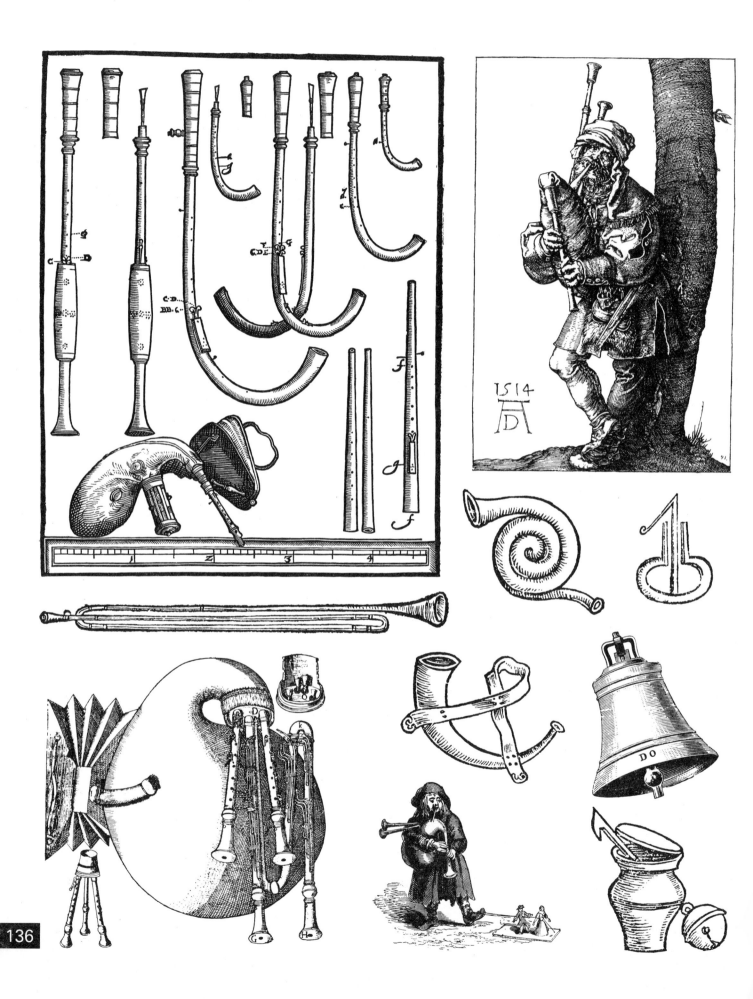

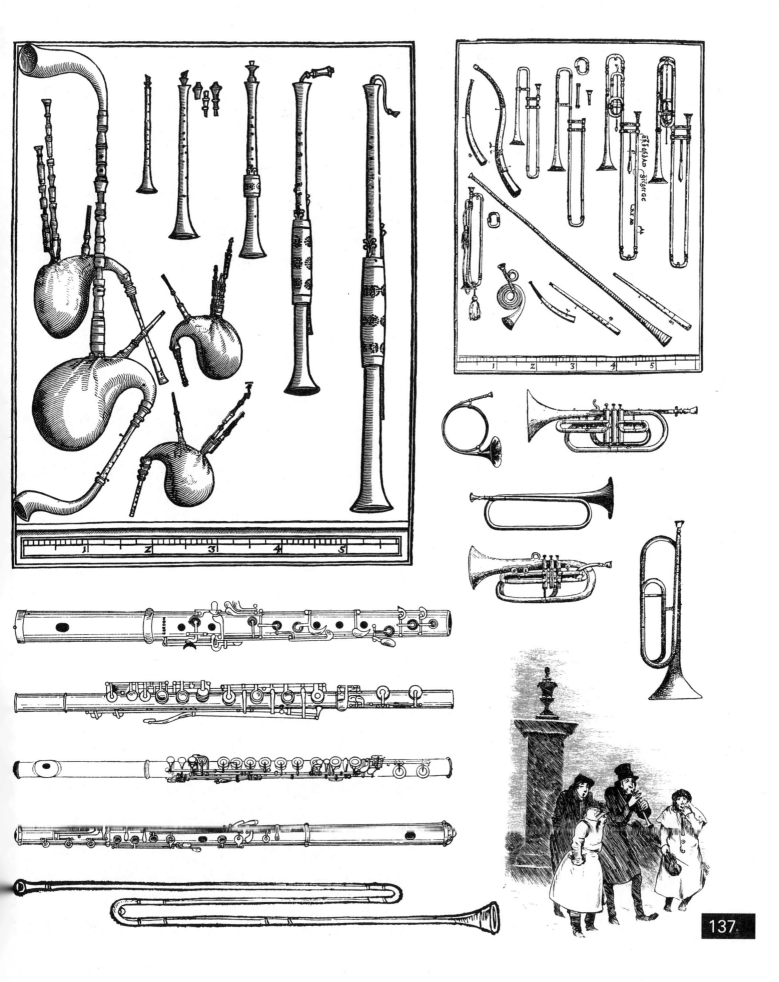

137

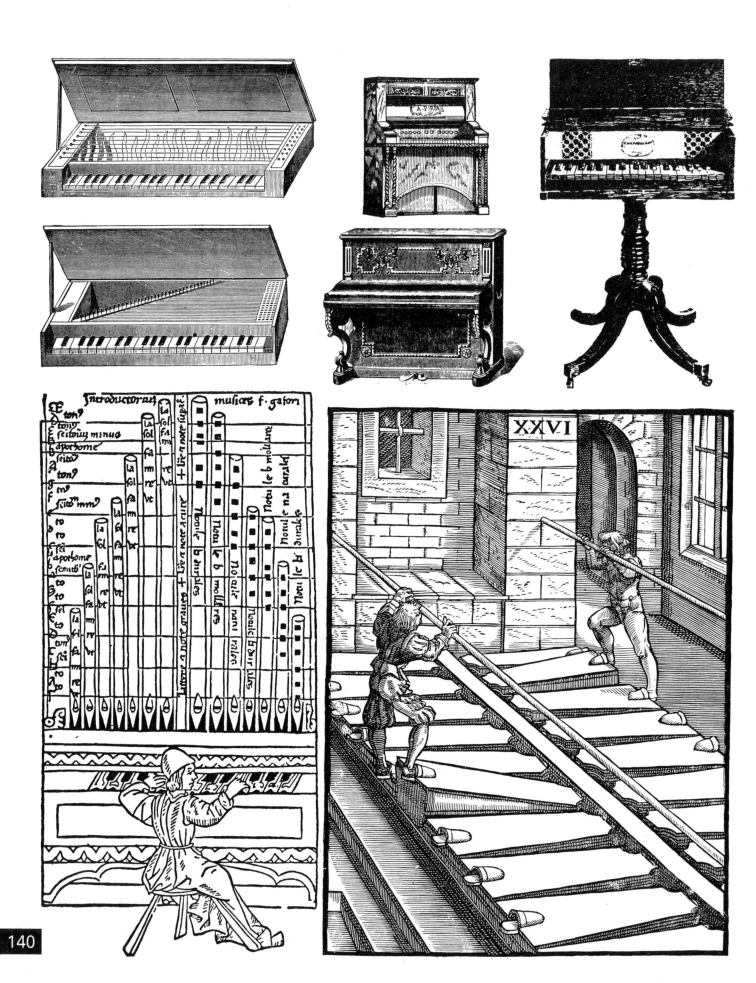

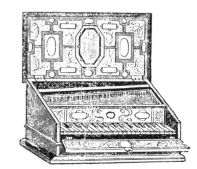

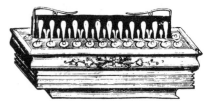

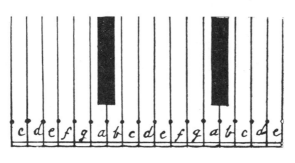

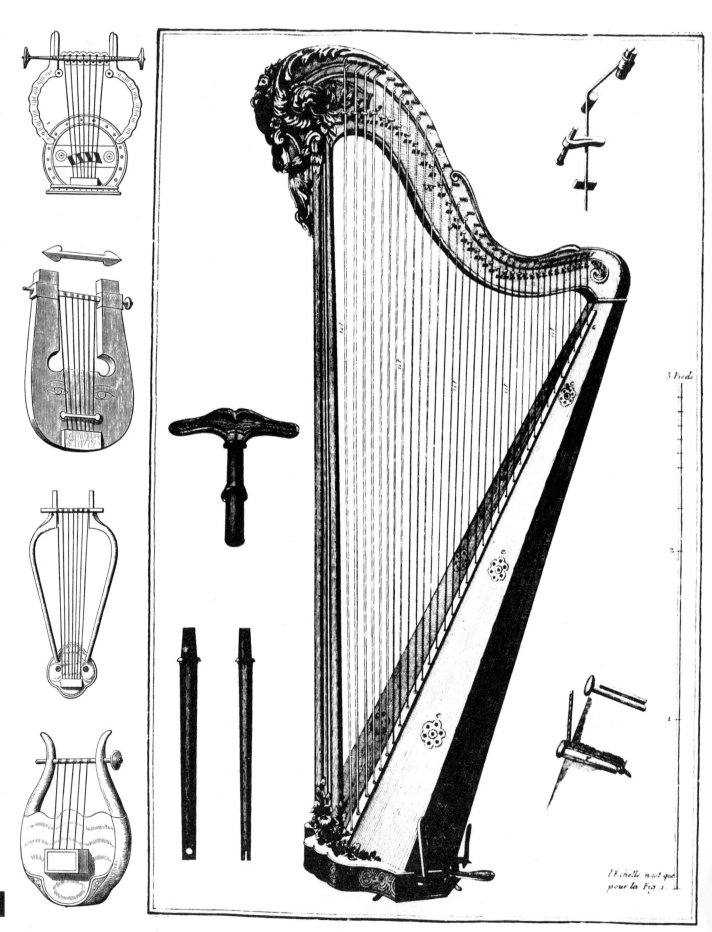

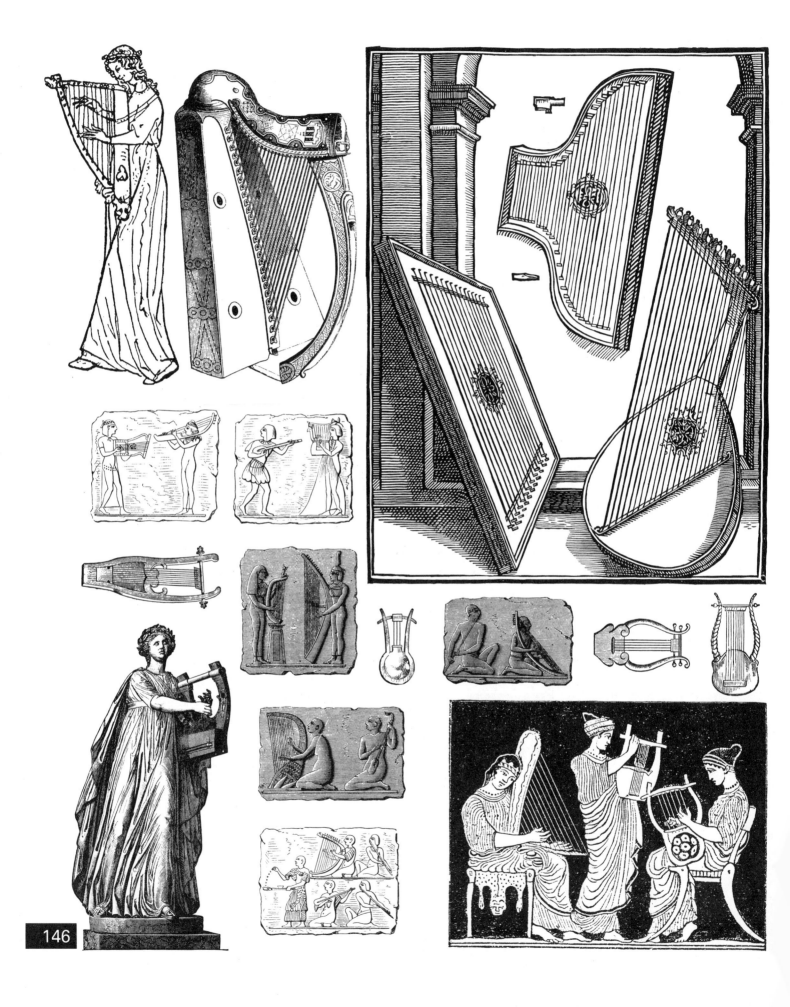

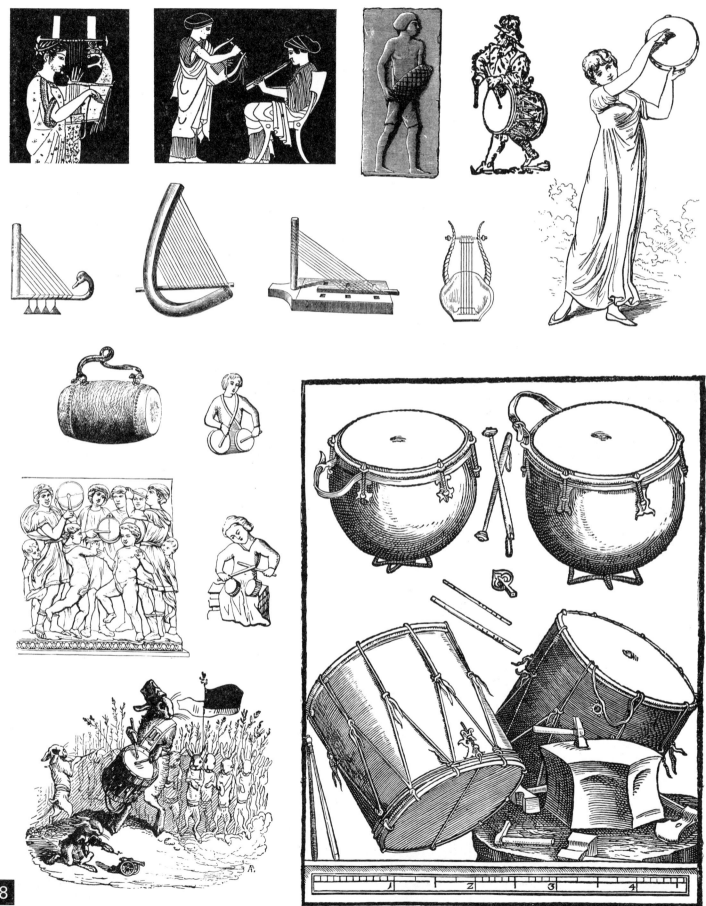

152

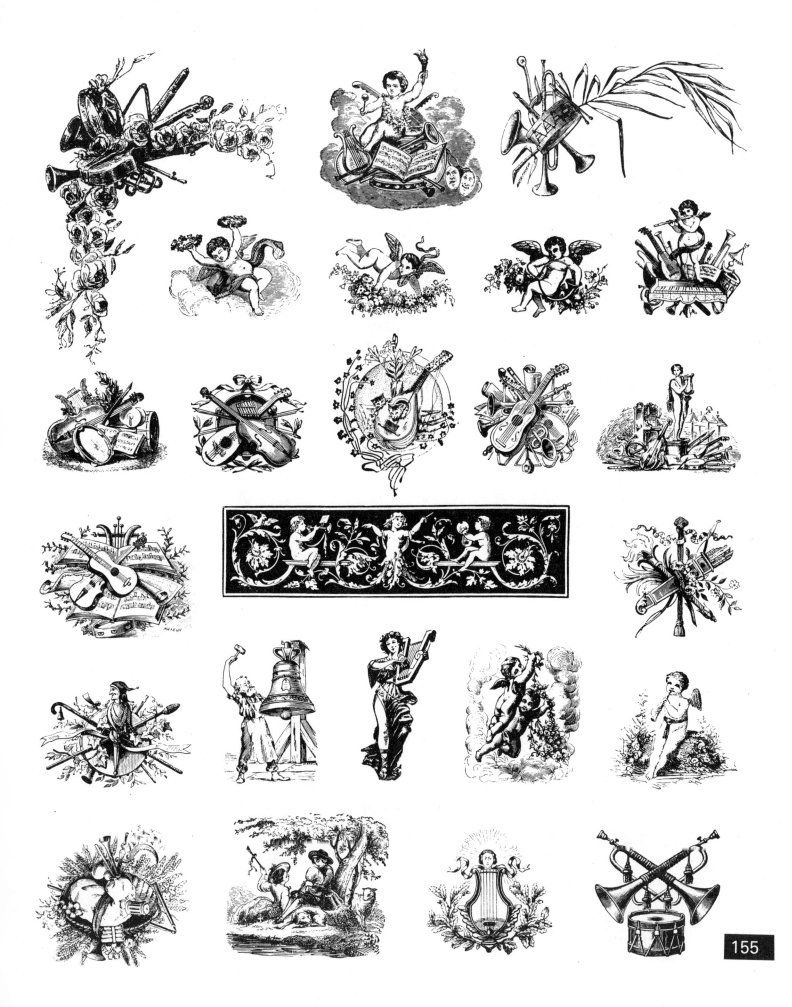

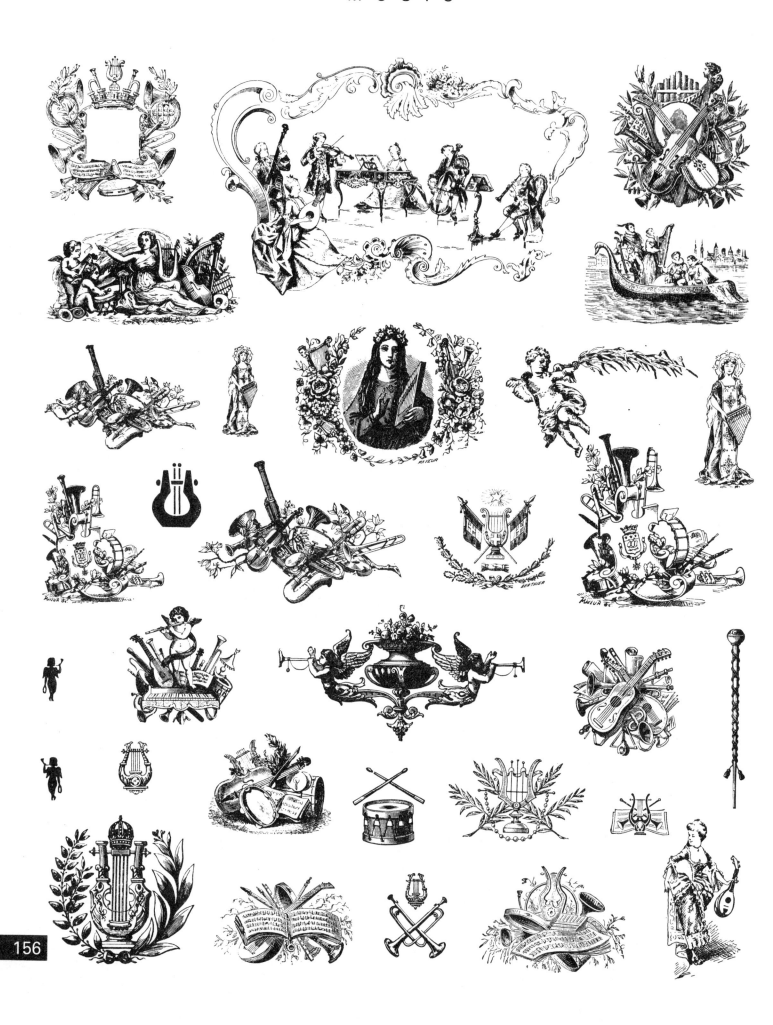

C·O·S·T·U·M·E

COSTUME

JOSEPHVS ROMANOR. IMPERATOR

162

167

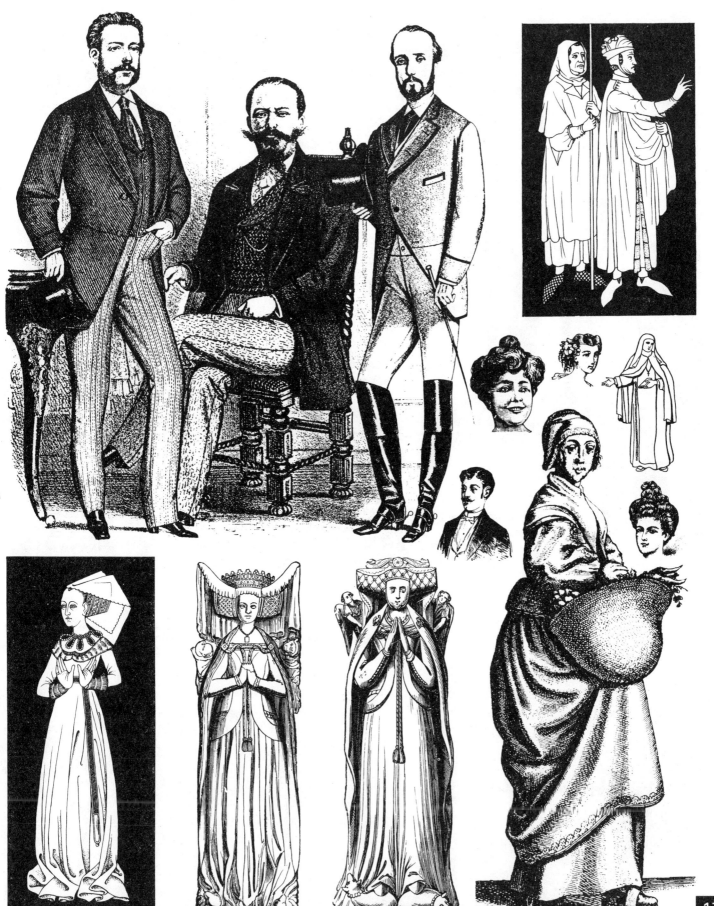

175

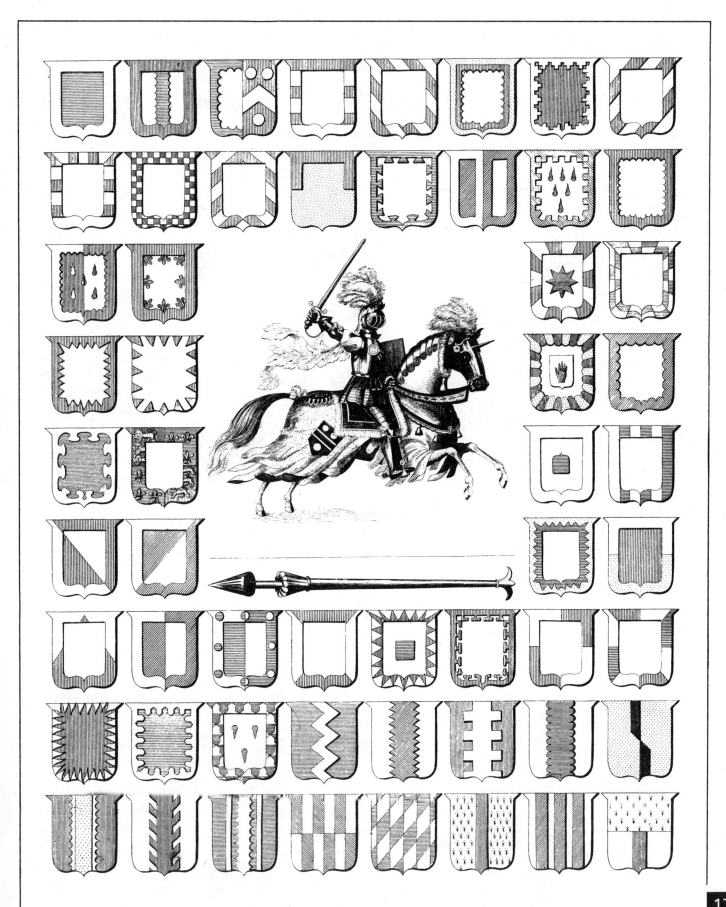

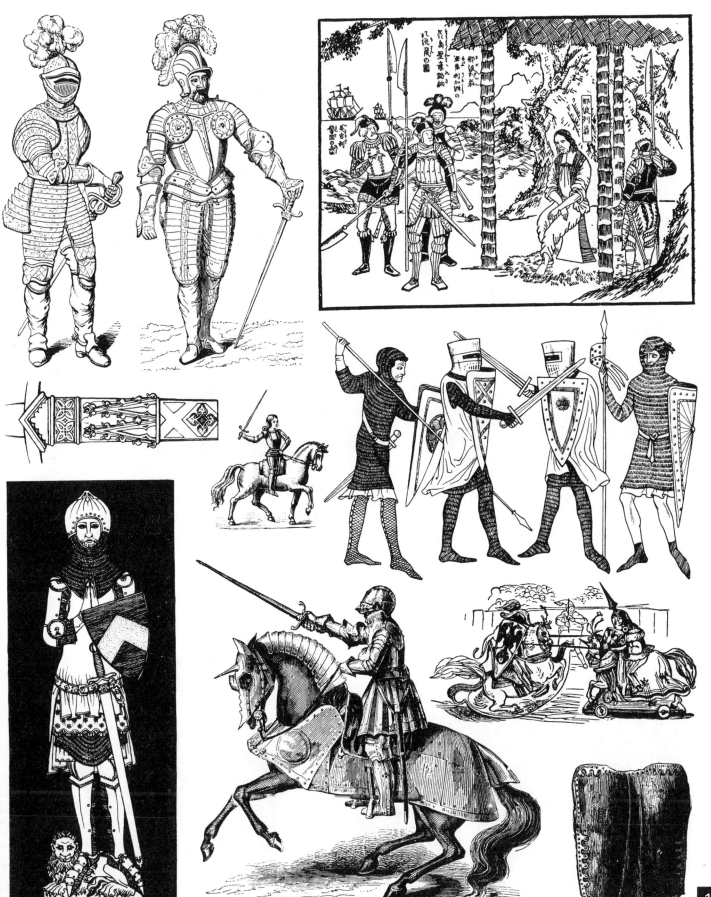

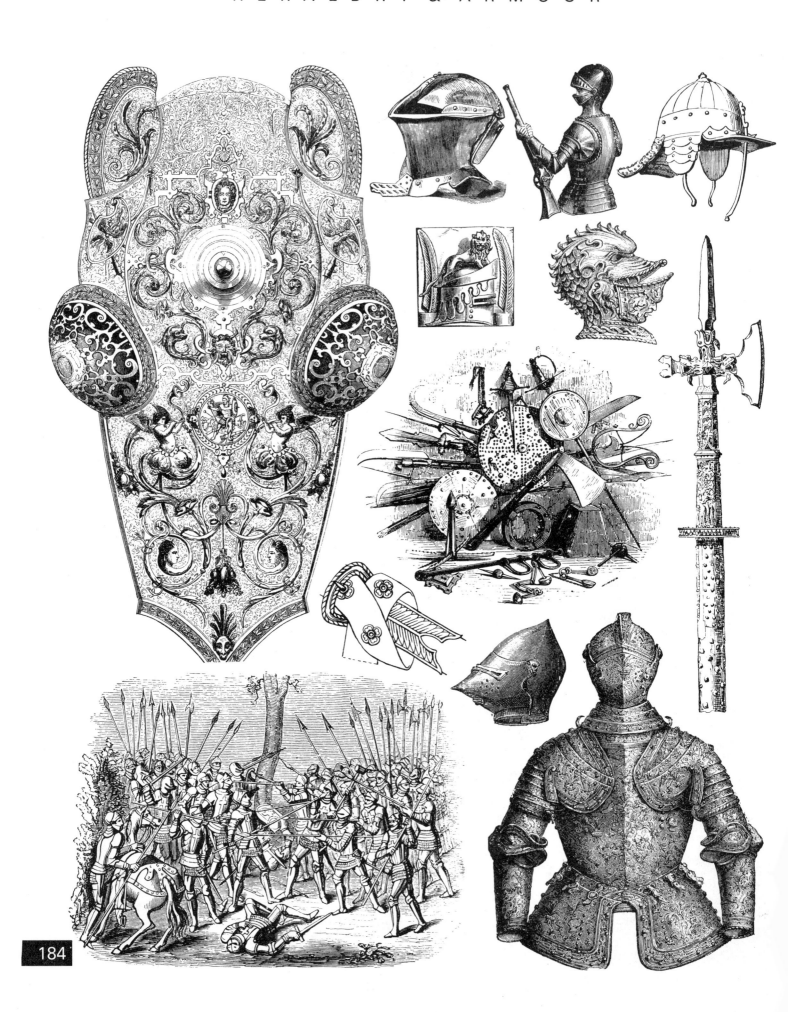

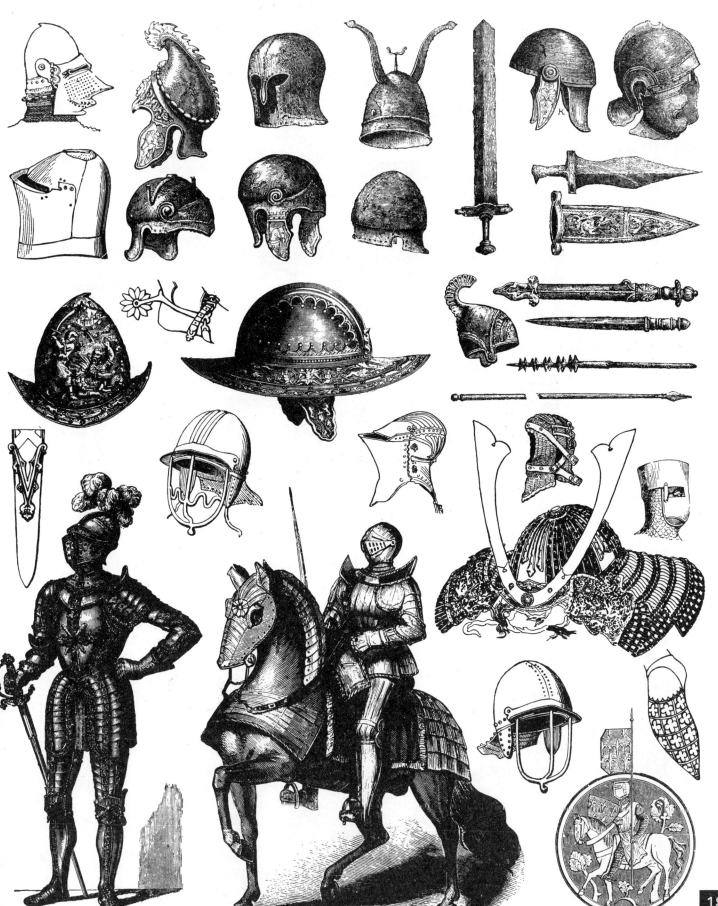

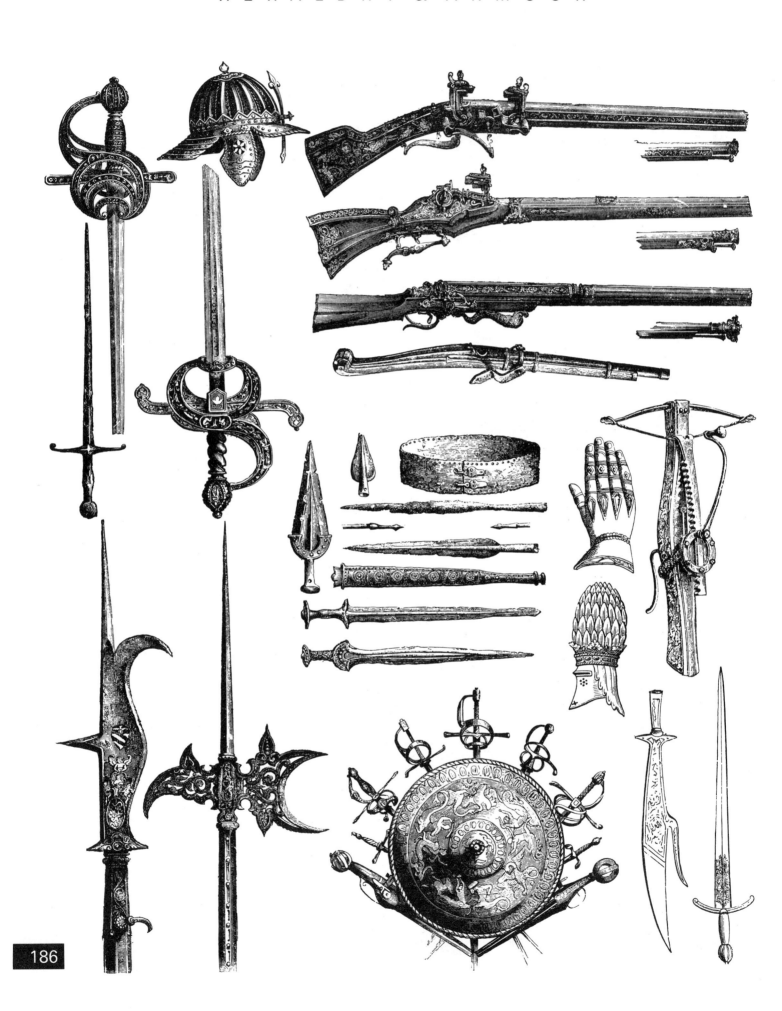

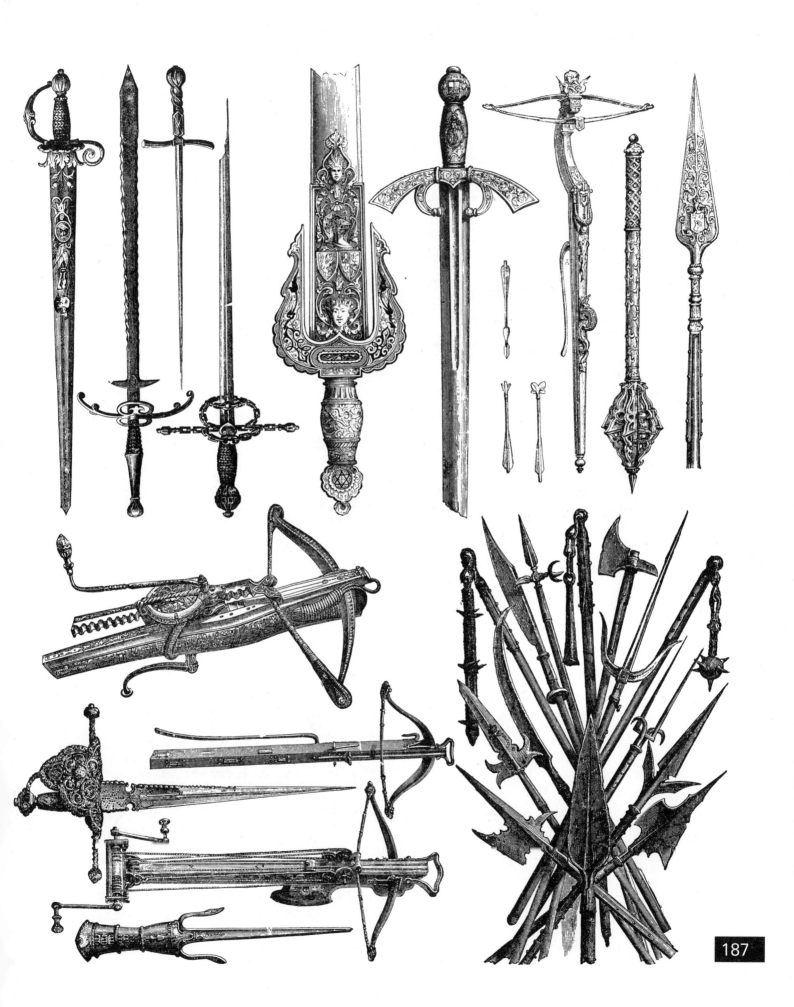

187

195

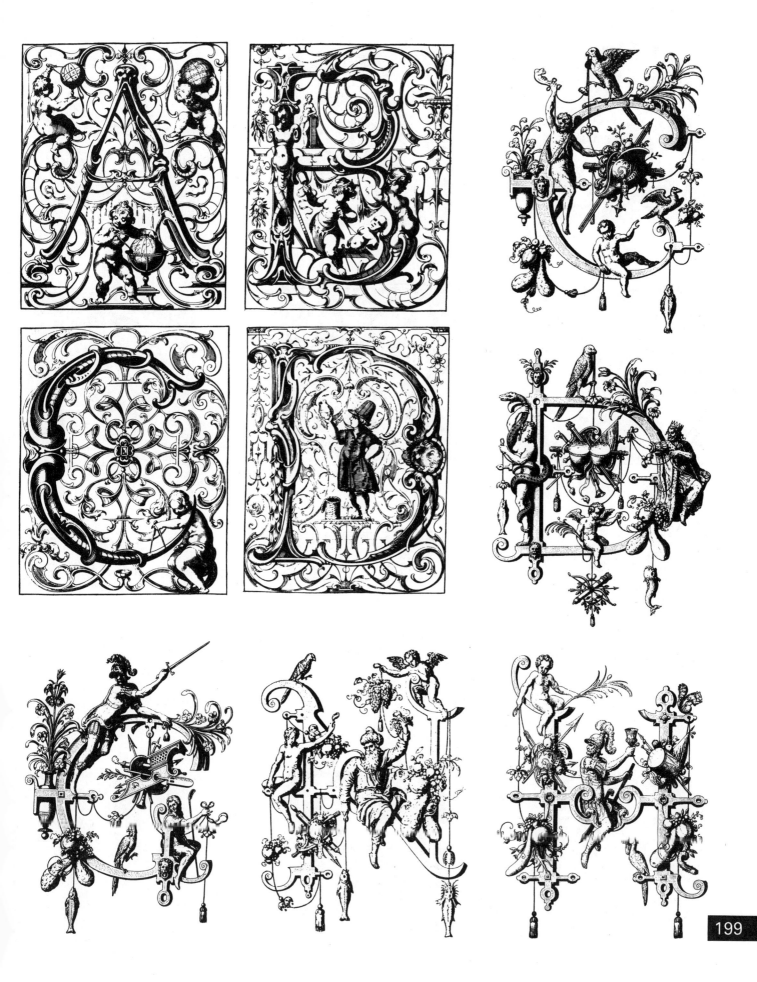

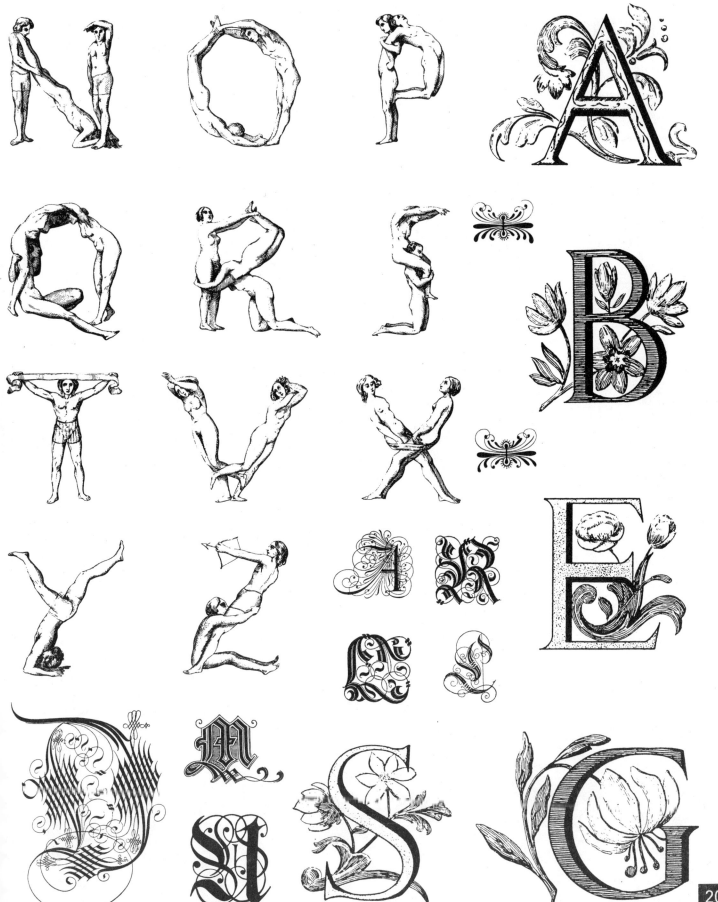

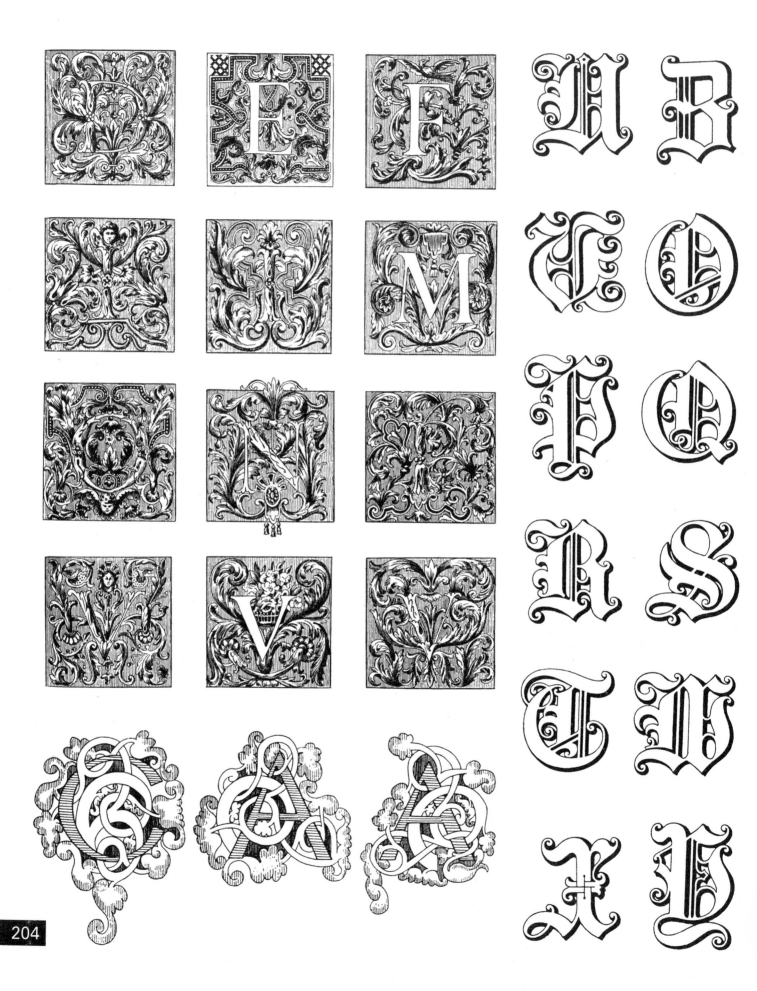

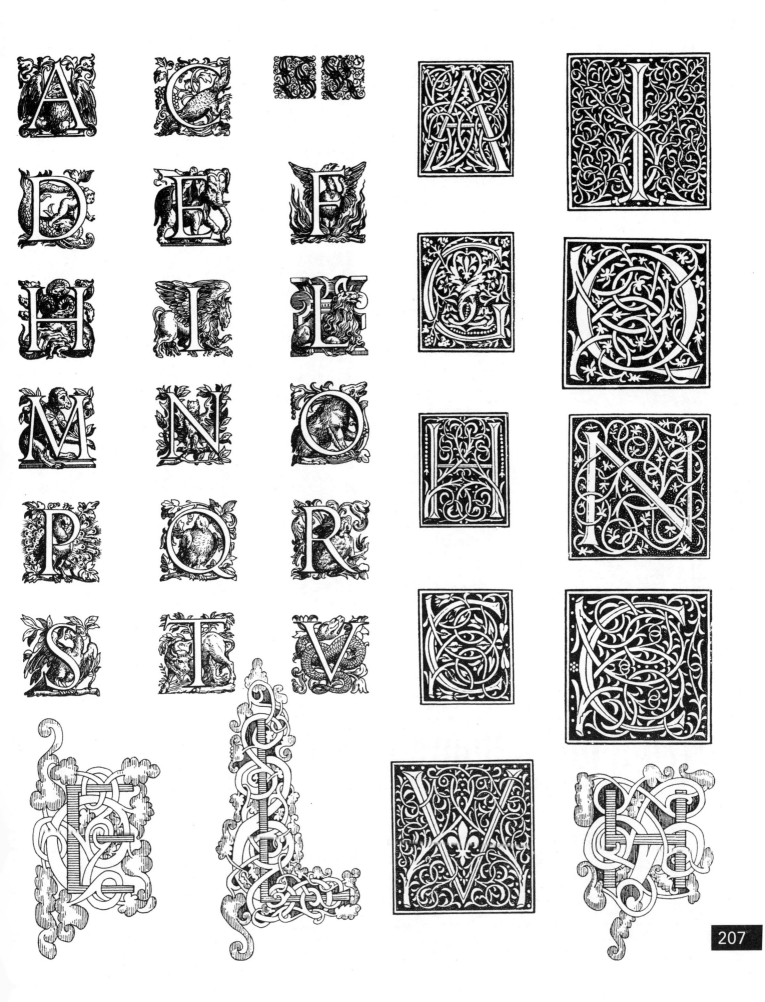

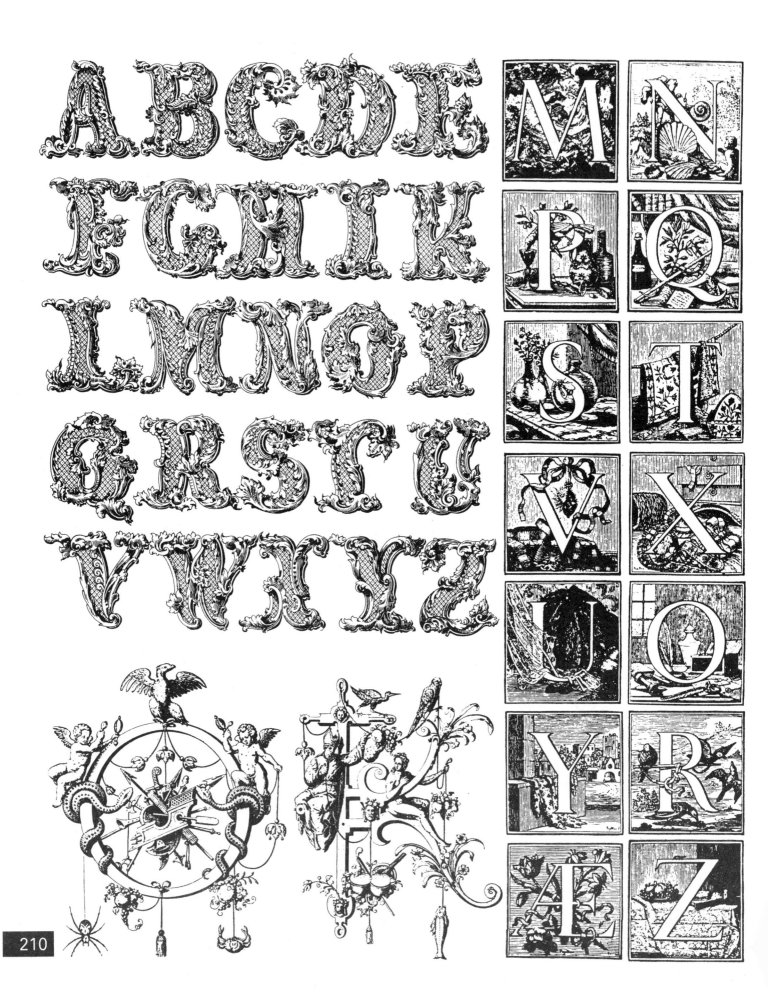

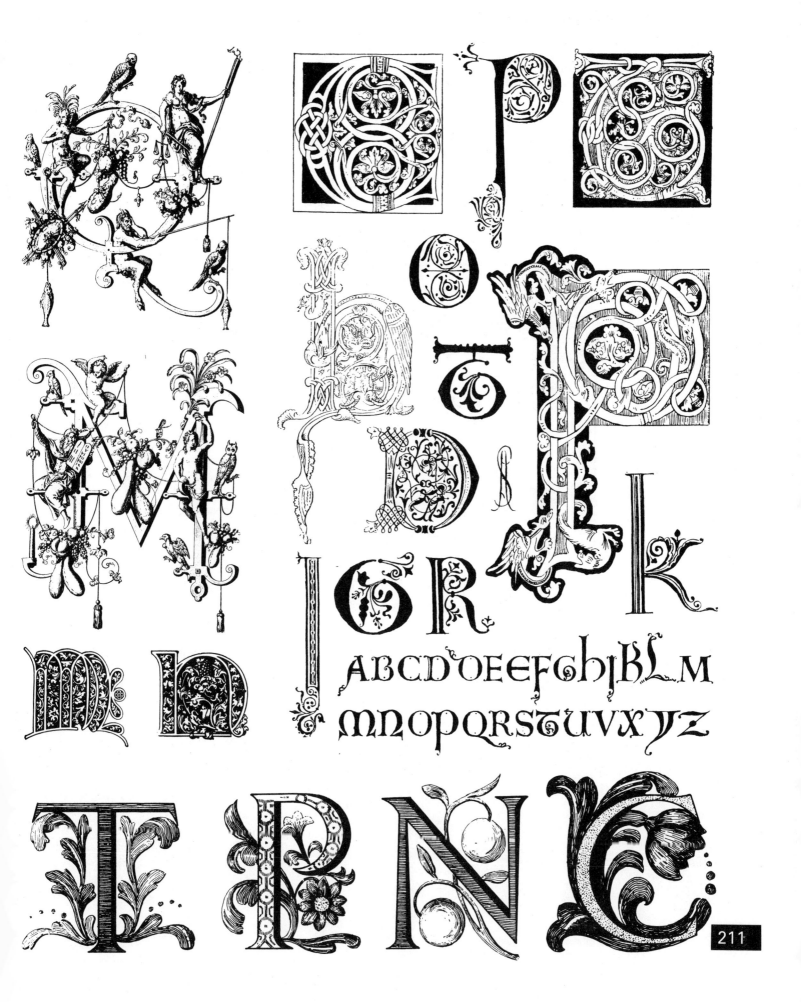

ABCDOEFGHIBLM
MNOPQRSTUVXYZ

211

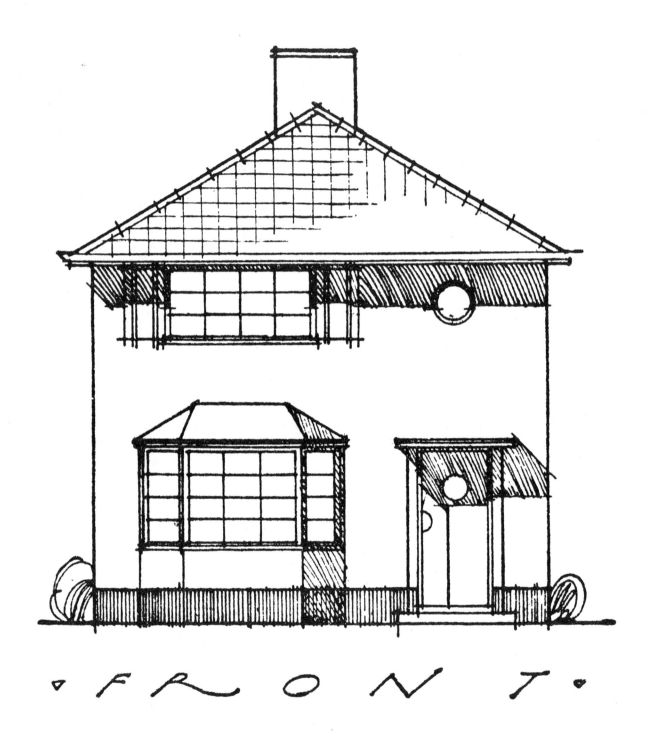

·F R O N T·

ARCHITECTURE

215

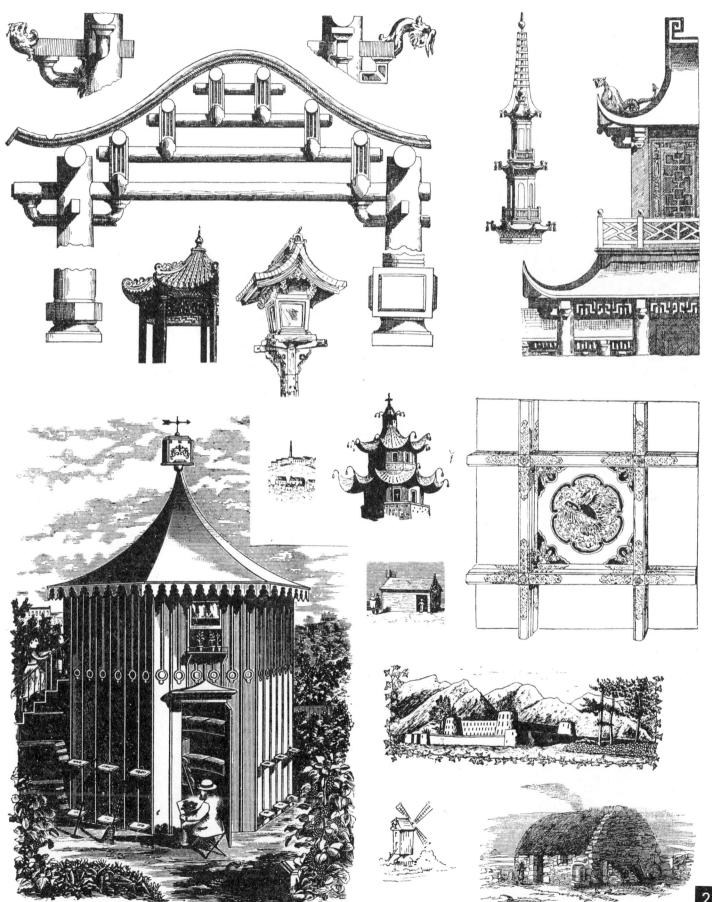

ARCHITECTURE

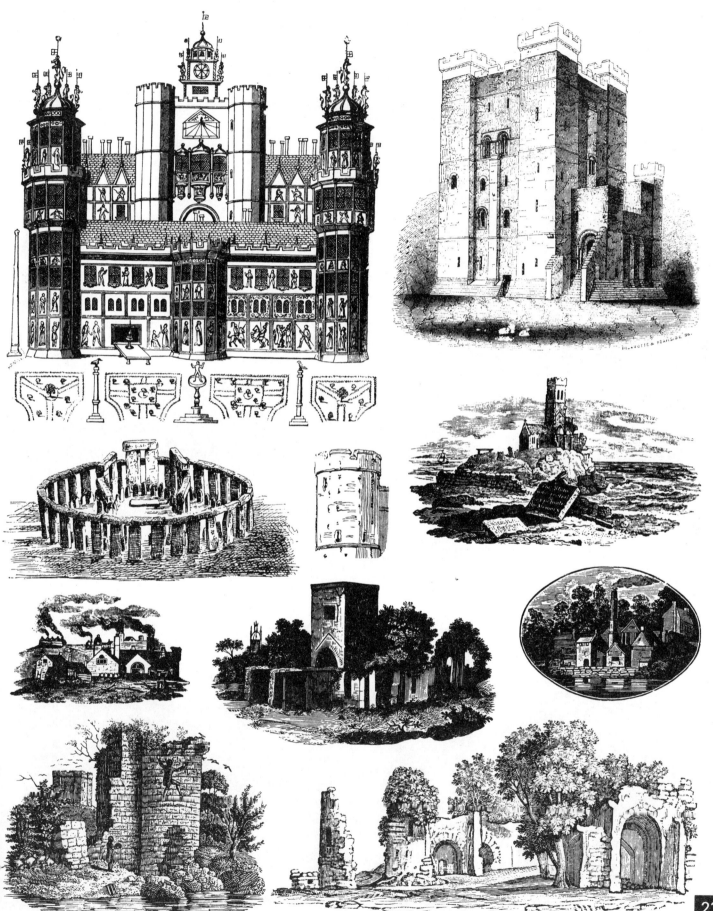

233

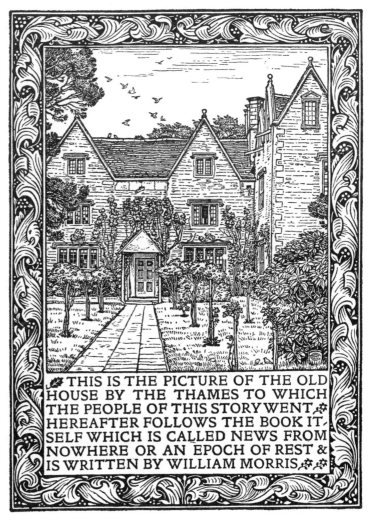

THIS IS THE PICTURE OF THE OLD HOUSE BY THE THAMES TO WHICH THE PEOPLE OF THIS STORY WENT. HEREAFTER FOLLOWS THE BOOK IT. SELF WHICH IS CALLED NEWS FROM NOWHERE OR AN EPOCH OF REST & IS WRITTEN BY WILLIAM MORRIS.

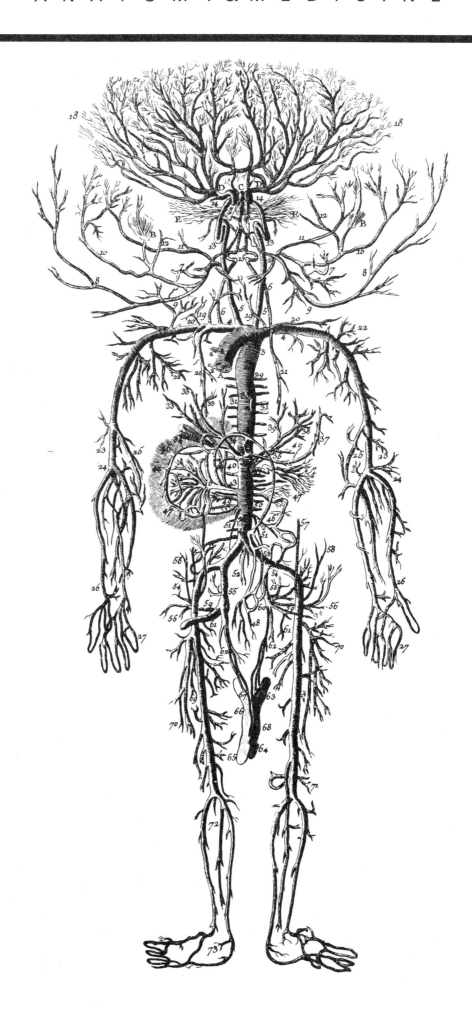

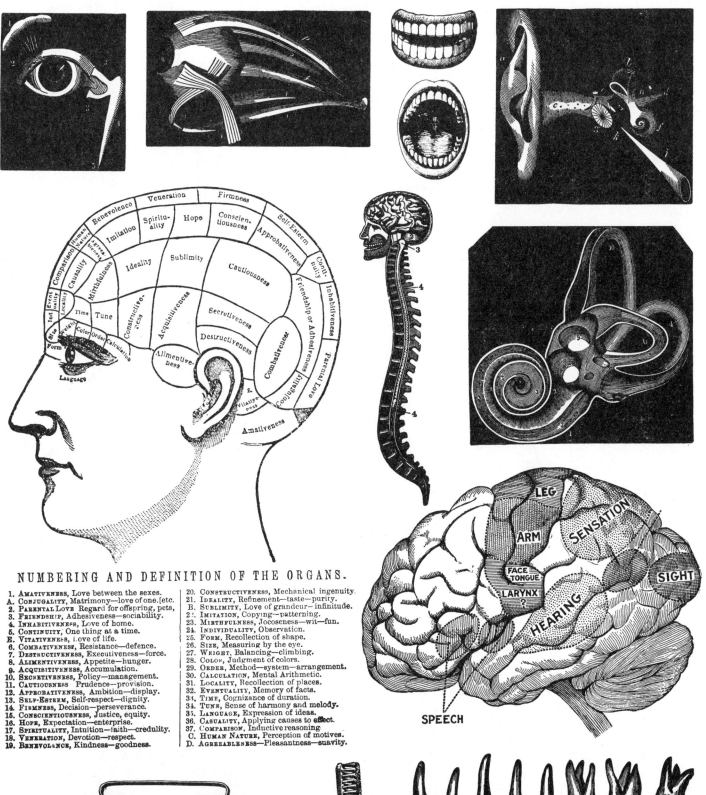

NUMBERING AND DEFINITION OF THE ORGANS.

1. **Amativeness**, Love between the sexes.
A. **Conjugality**, Matrimony—love of one. [etc.
2. **Parental Love** Regard for offspring, pets,
3. **Friendship**, Adhesiveness—sociability.
4. **Inhabitiveness**, Love of home.
5. **Continuity**, One thing at a time.
E. **Vitativeness**, Love of life.
6. **Combativeness**, Resistance—defence.
7. **Destructiveness**, Executiveness—force.
8. **Alimentiveness**, Appetite—hunger.
9. **Acquisitiveness**, Accumulation.
10. **Secretiveness**, Policy—management.
11. **Cautiousness** Prudence—provision.
12. **Approbativeness**, Ambition—display.
13. **Self-Esteem**, Self-respect—dignity.
14. **Firmness**, Decision—perseverance.
15. **Conscientiousness**, Justice, equity.
16. **Hope**, Expectation—enterprise.
17. **Spirituality**, Intuition—faith—credulity.
18. **Veneration**, Devotion—respect.
19. **Benevolence**, Kindness—goodness.

20. **Constructiveness**, Mechanical ingenuity.
21. **Ideality**, Refinement—taste—purity.
B. **Sublimity**, Love of grandeur—infinitude.
22. **Imitation**, Copying—patterning.
23. **Mirthfulness**, Jocoseness—wit—fun.
24. **Individuality**, Observation.
25. **Form**, Recollection of shape.
26. **Size**, Measuring by the eye.
27. **Weight**, Balancing—climbing.
28. **Color**, Judgment of colors.
29. **Order**, Method—system—arrangement.
30. **Calculation**, Mental Arithmetic.
31. **Locality**, Recollection of places.
32. **Eventuality**, Memory of facts.
33. **Time**, Cognizance of duration.
34. **Tune**, Sense of harmony and melody.
35. **Language**, Expression of ideas.
36. **Casuality**, Applying causes to effect.
37. **Comparison**, Inductive reasoning
C. **Human Nature**, Perception of motives.
D. **Agreeableness**—Pleasantness—suavity.

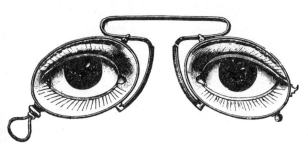

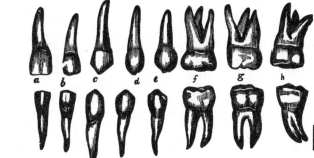

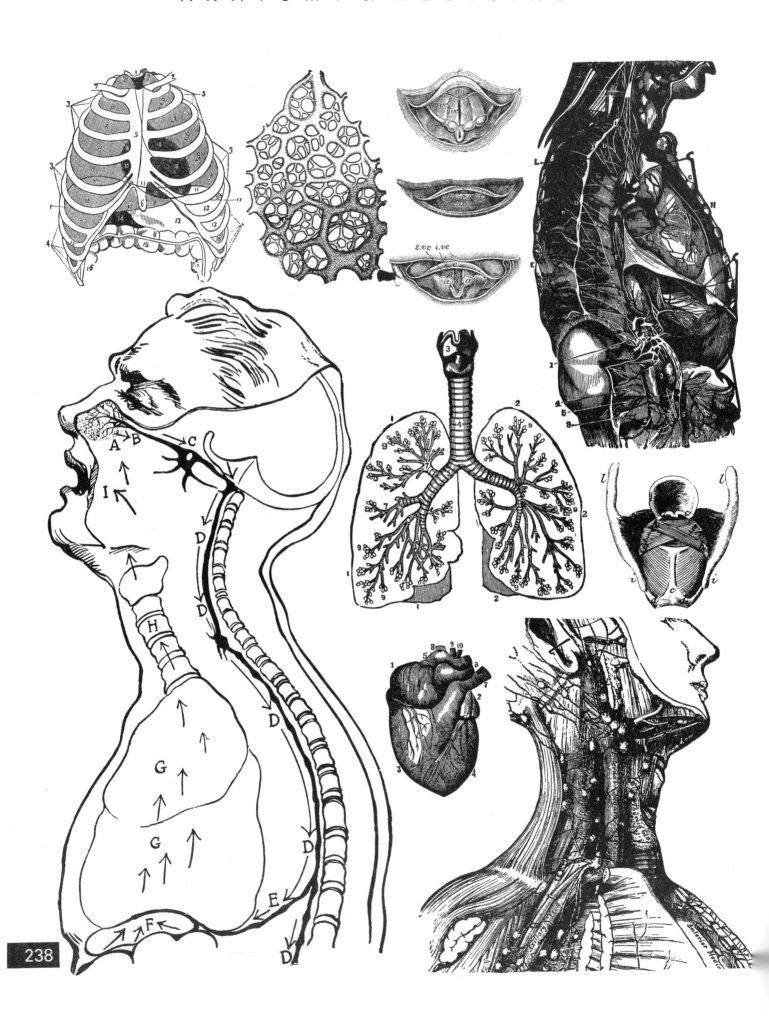

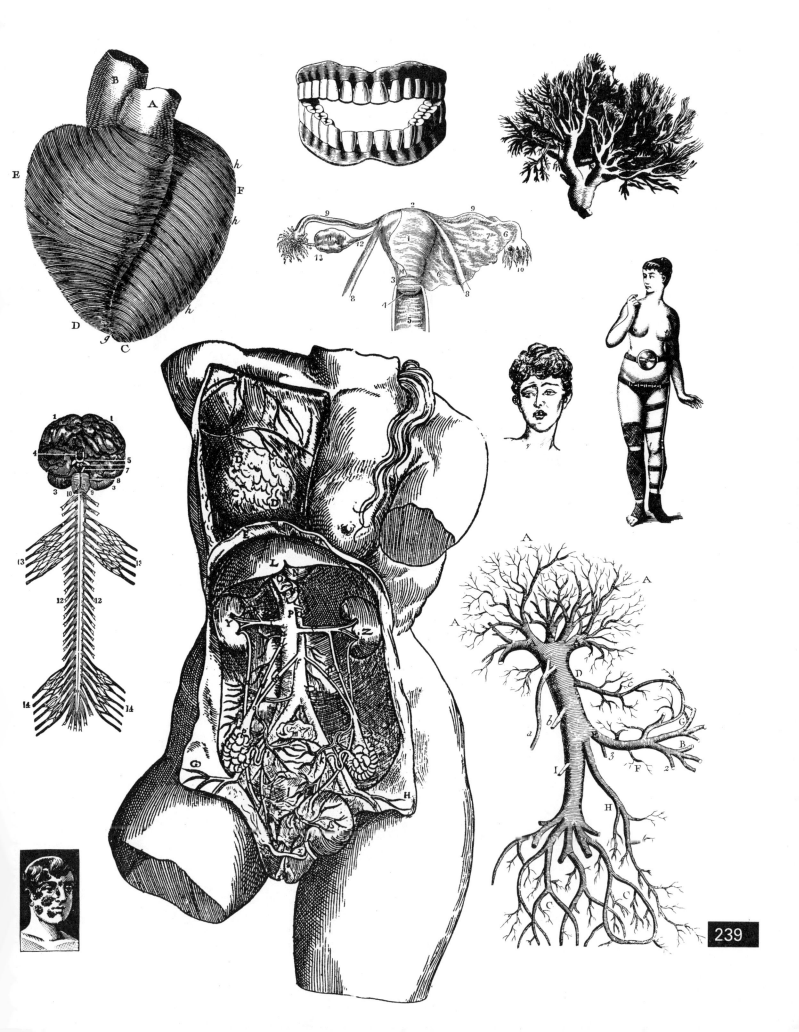

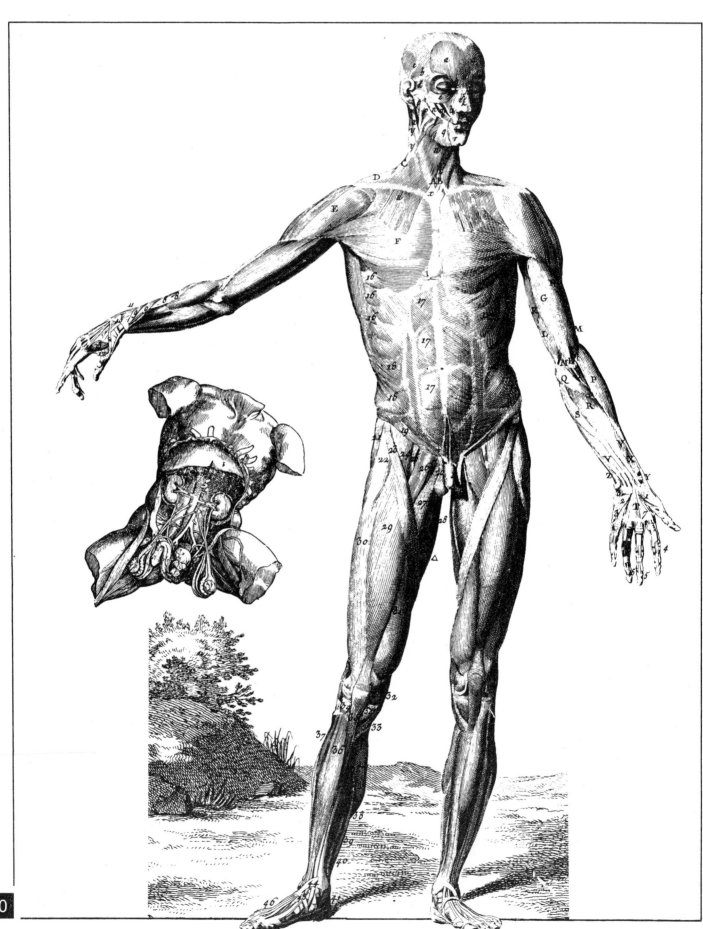

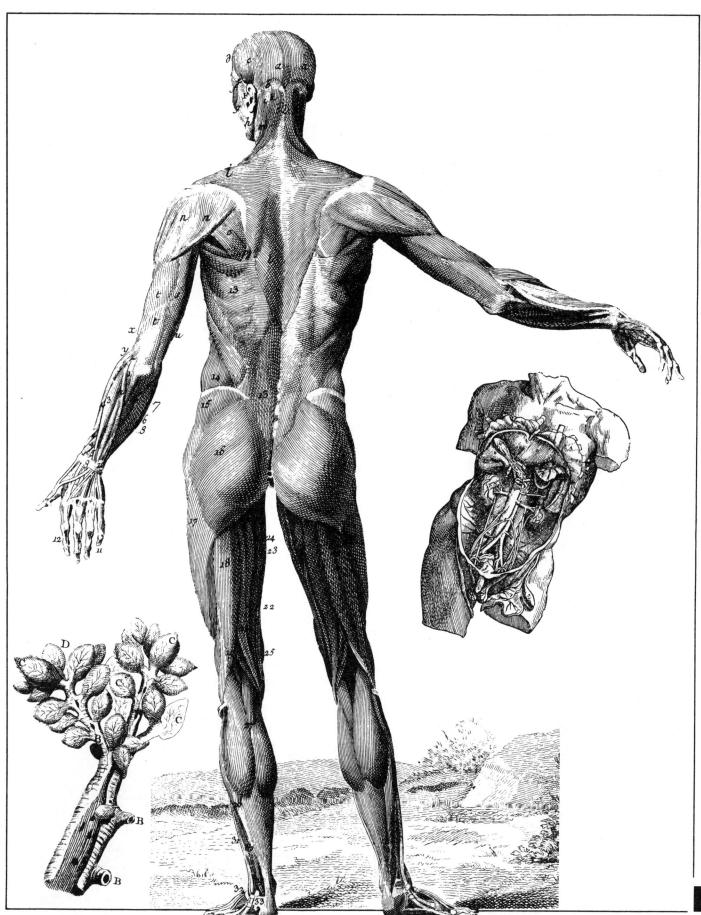

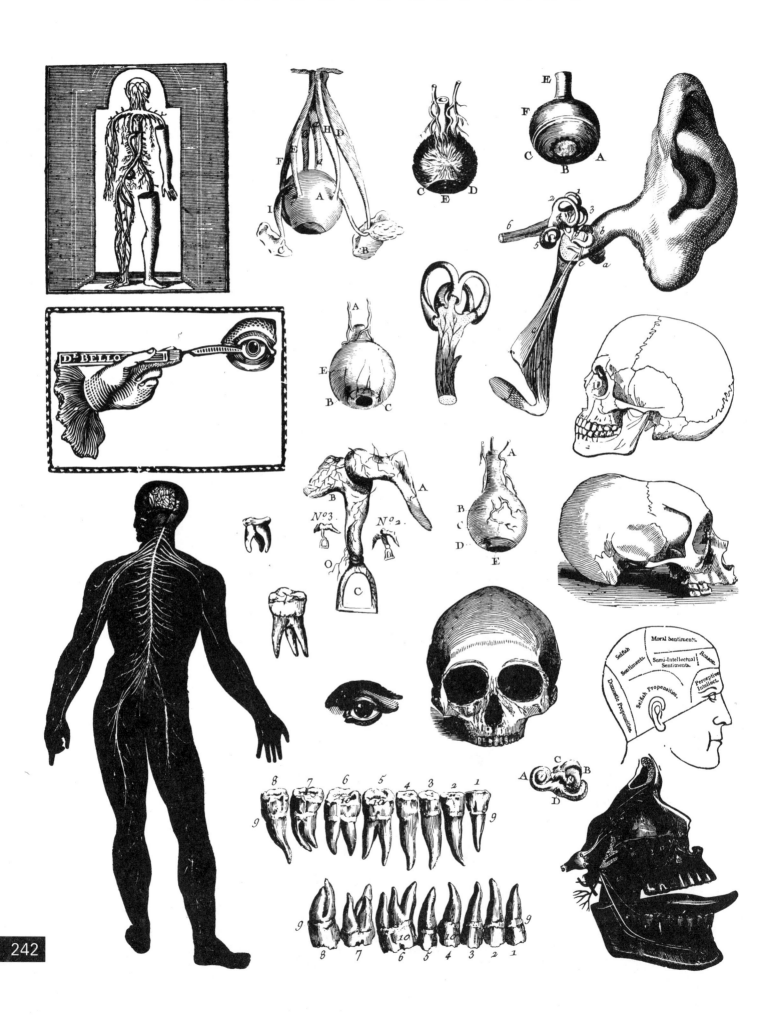

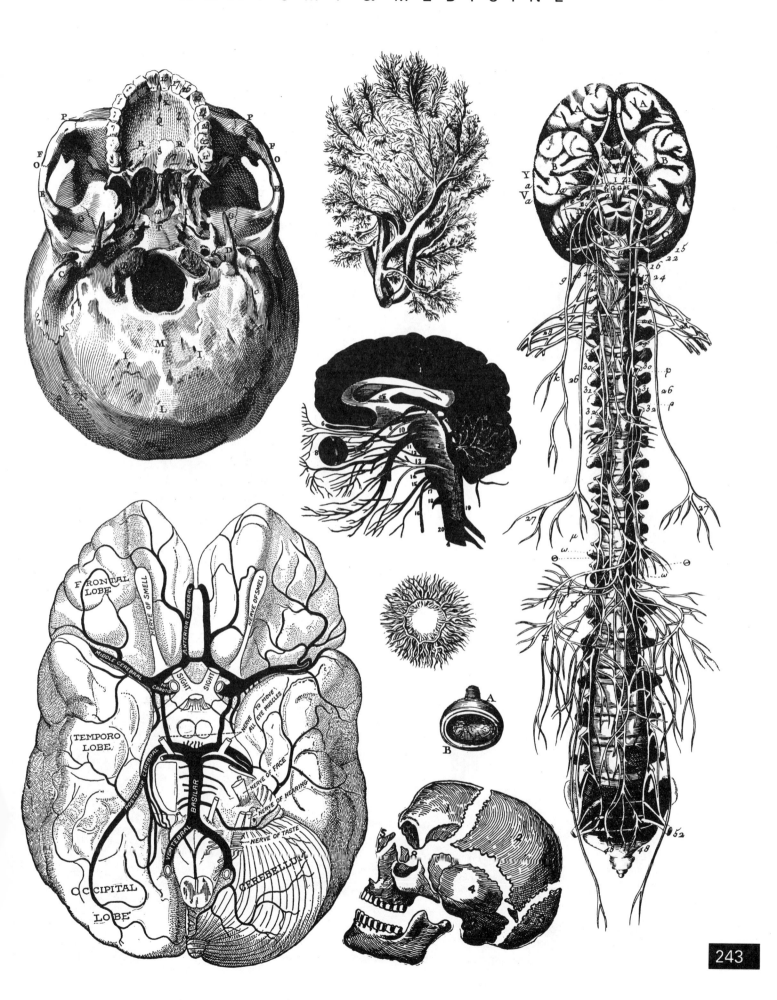

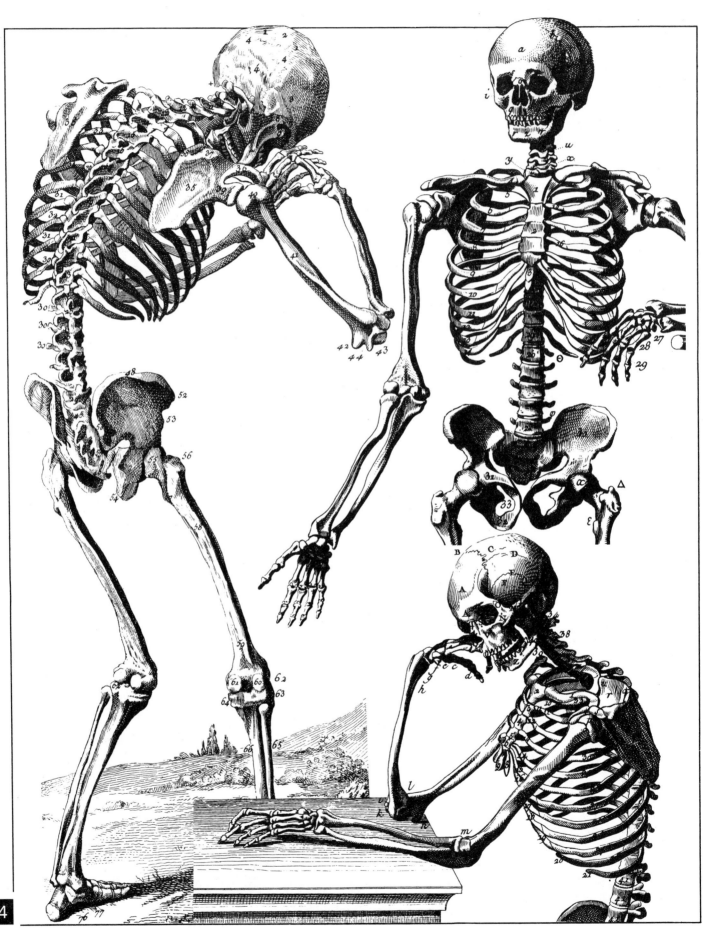

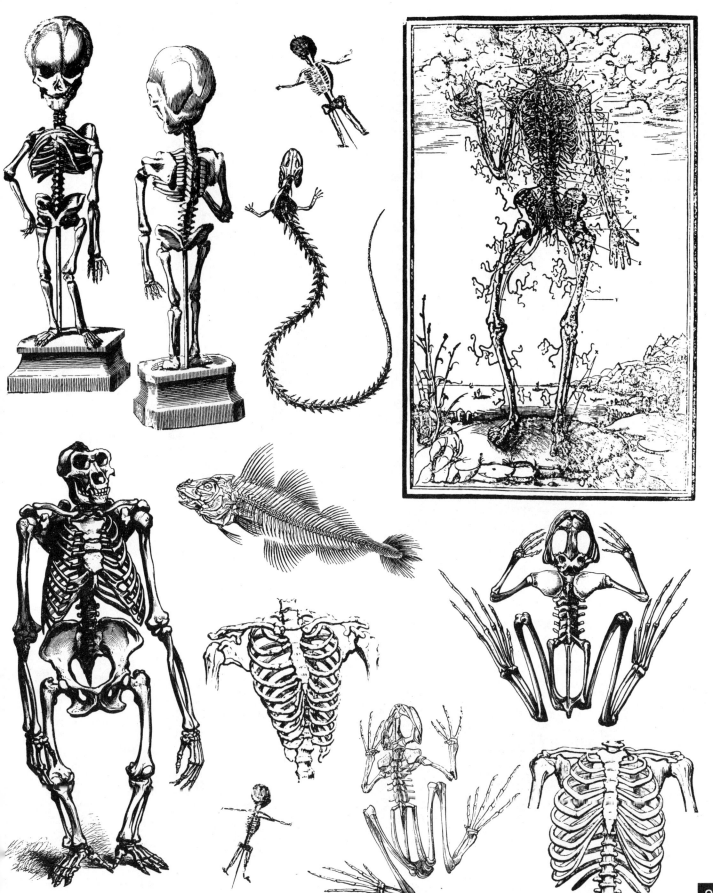

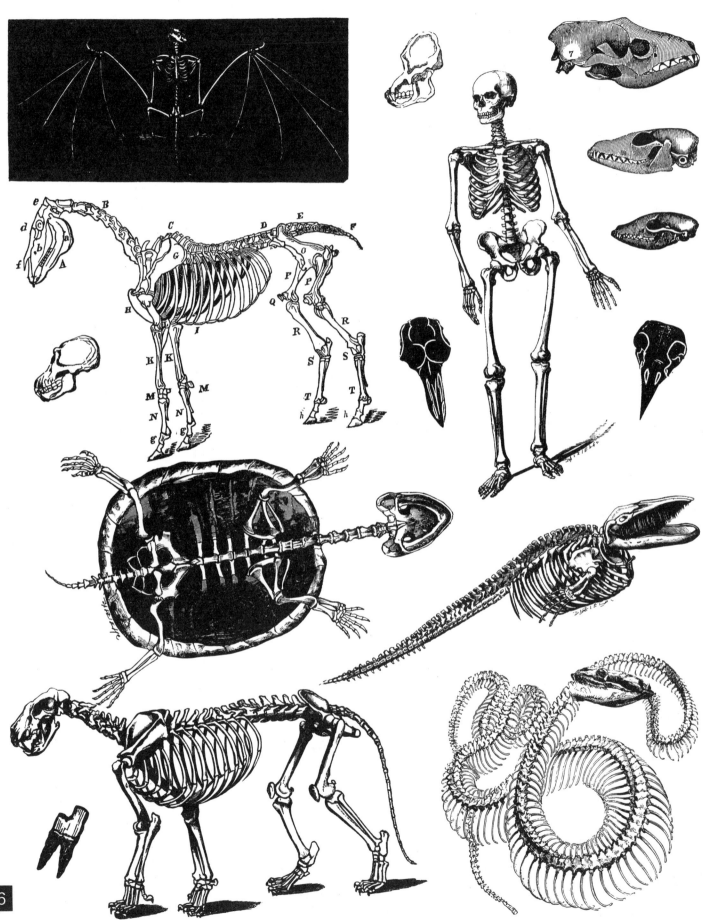

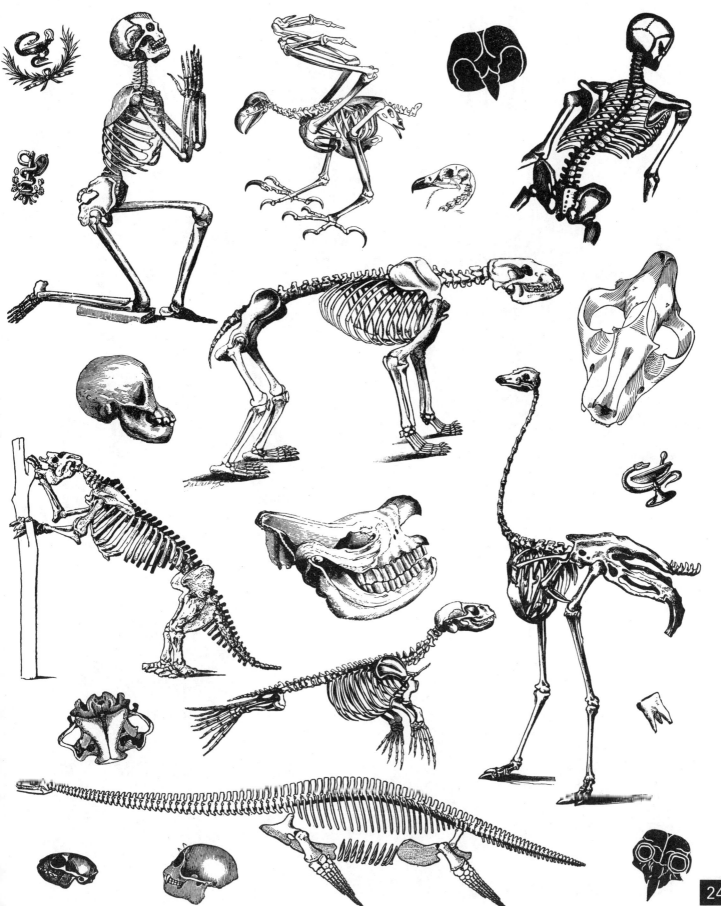

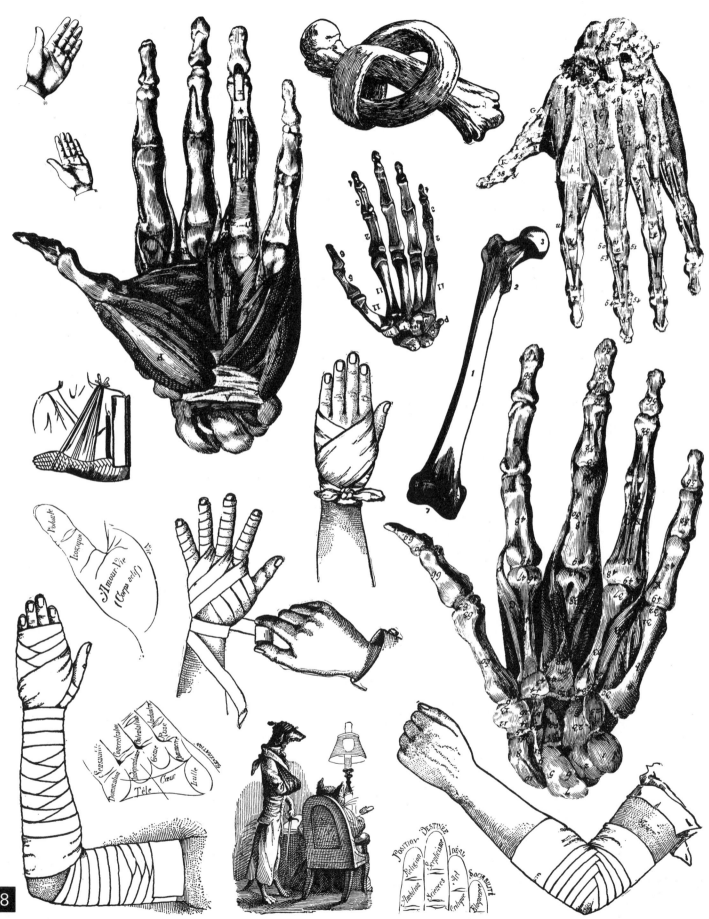

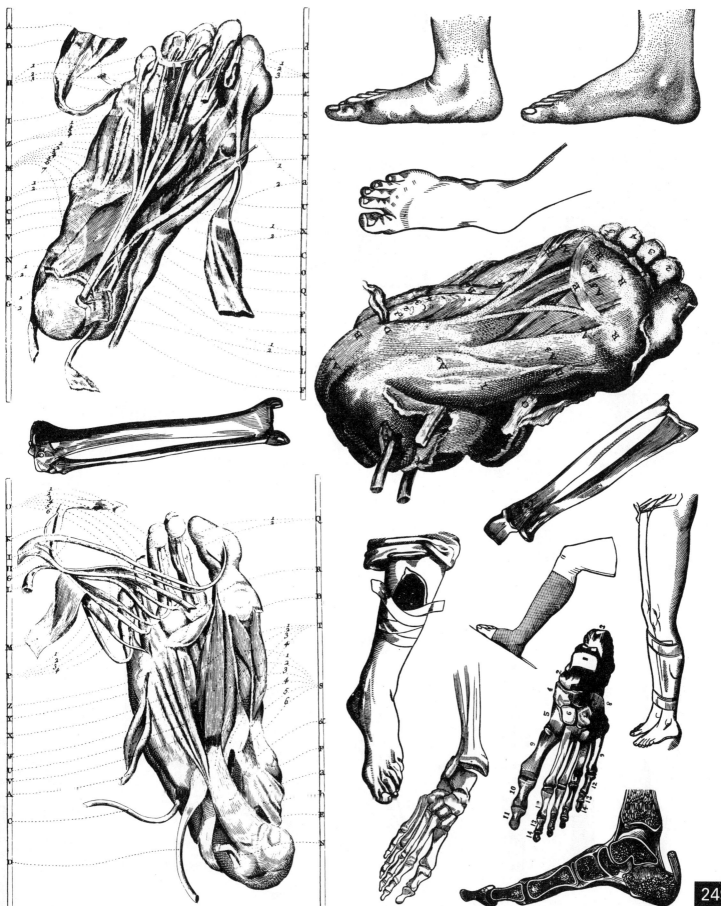

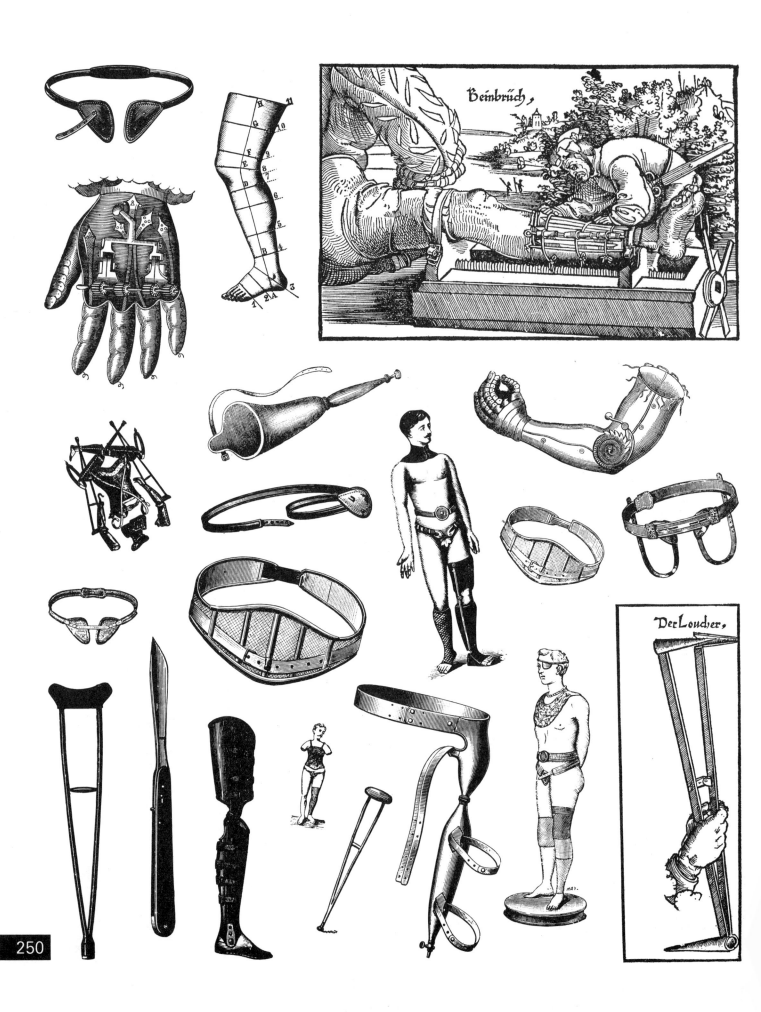

Beinbrüch,

Der Loucher,

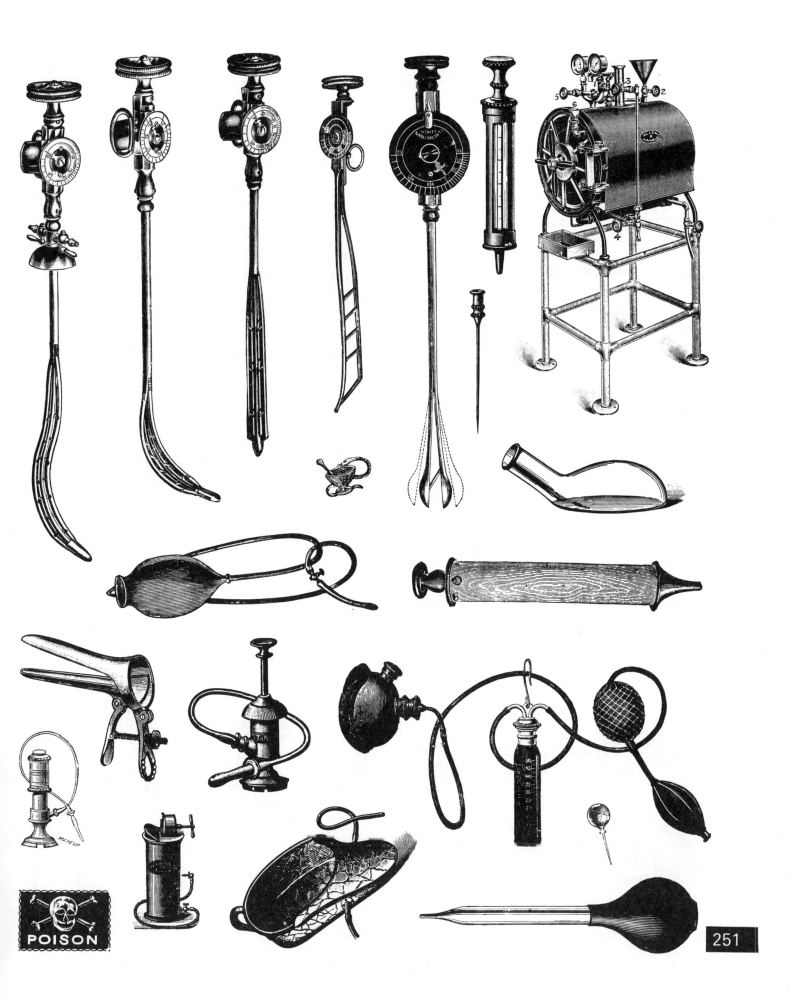

POISON

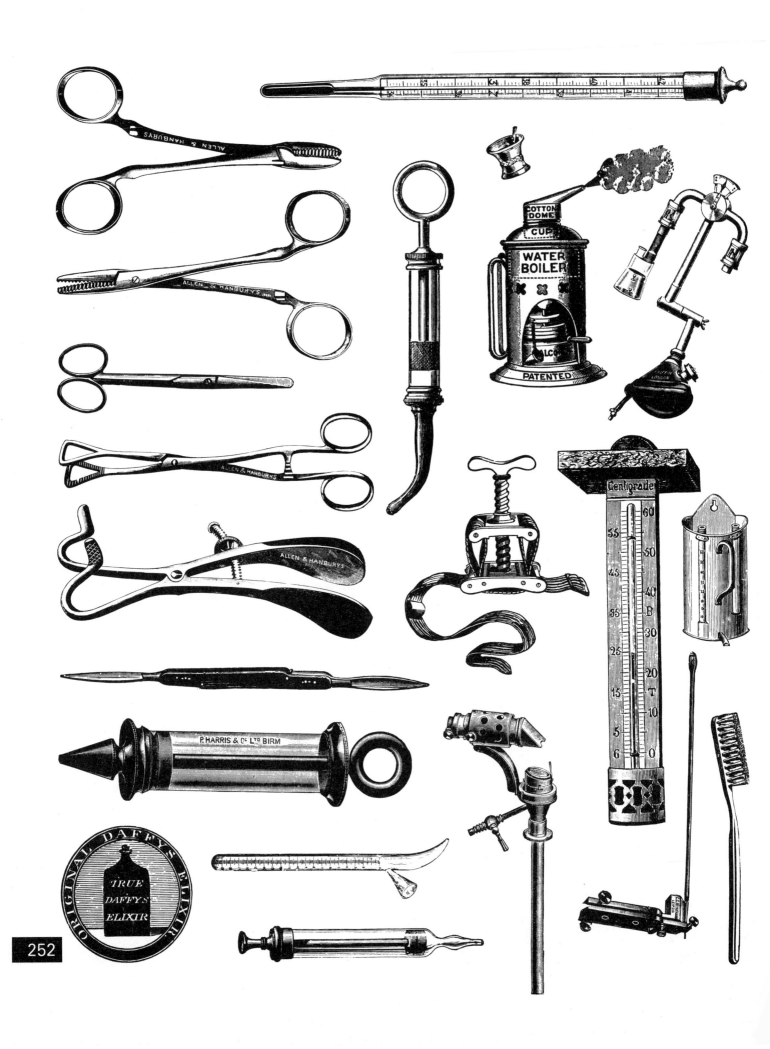

252

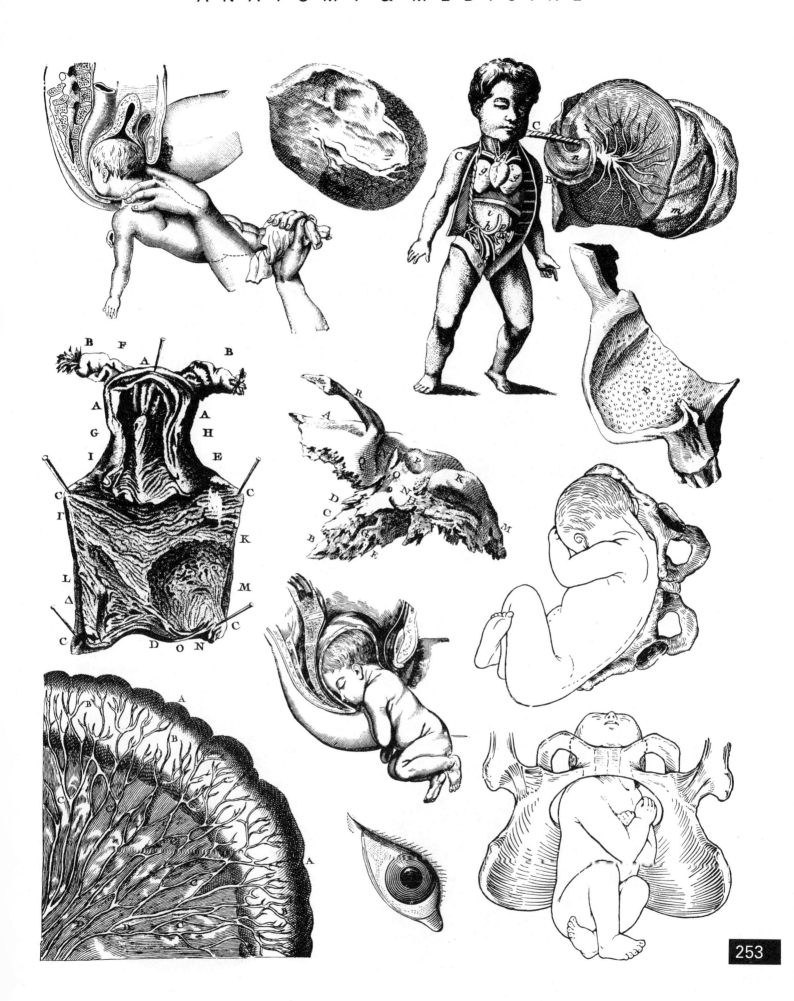

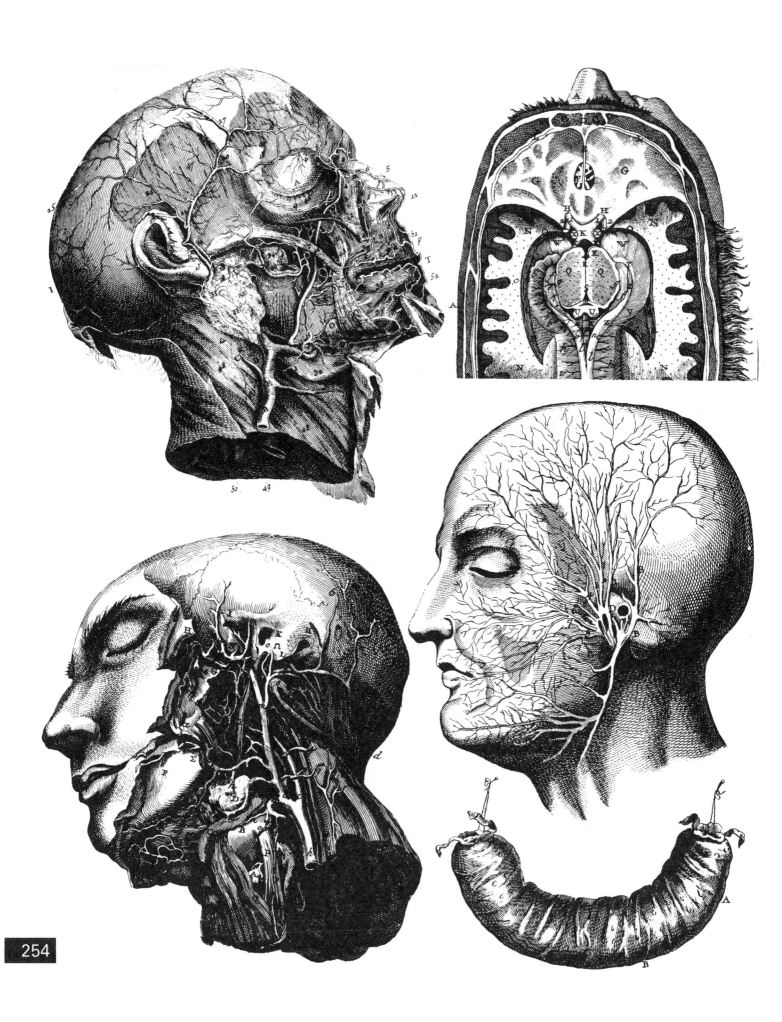

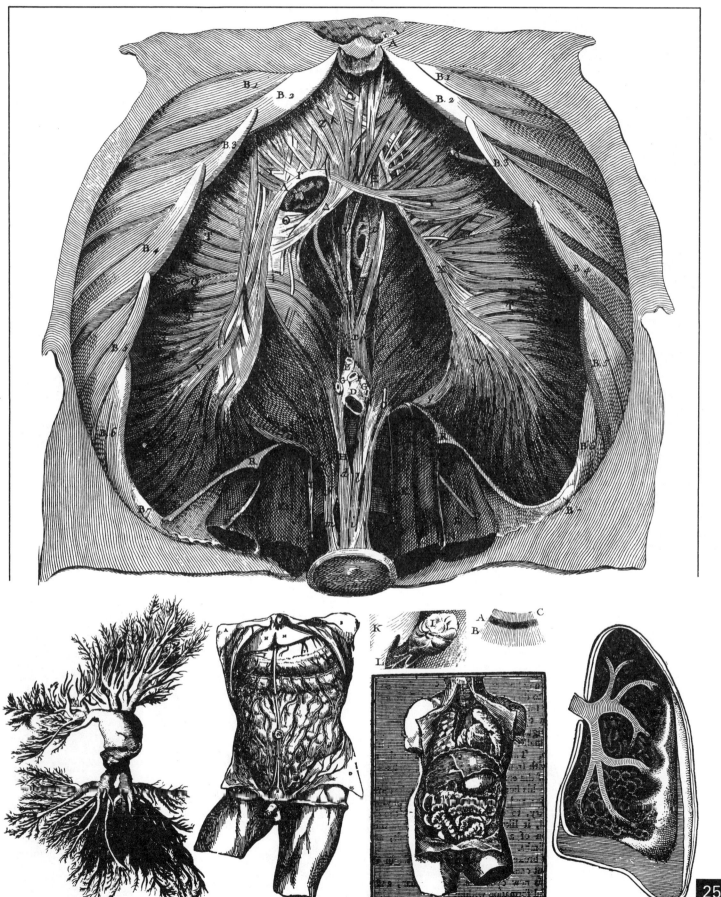

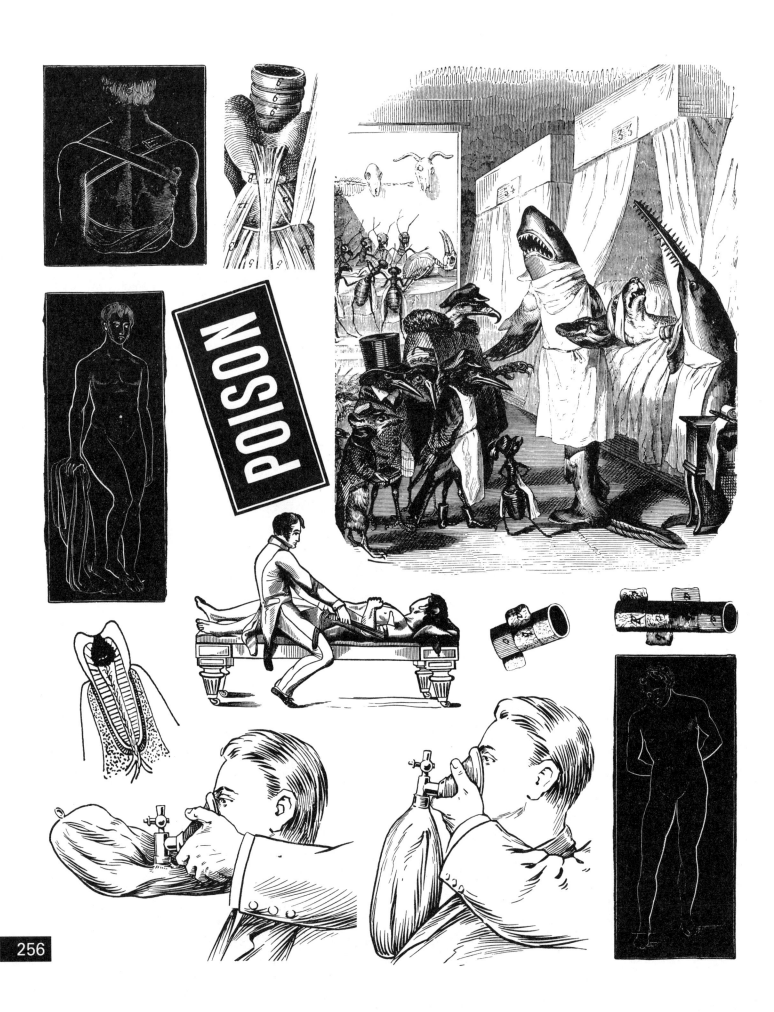

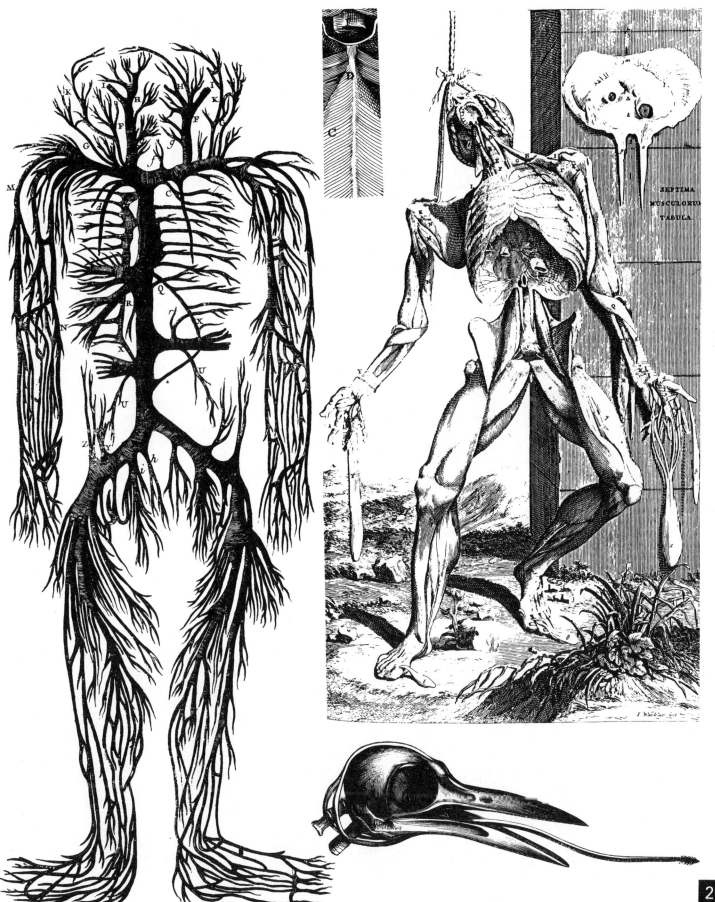

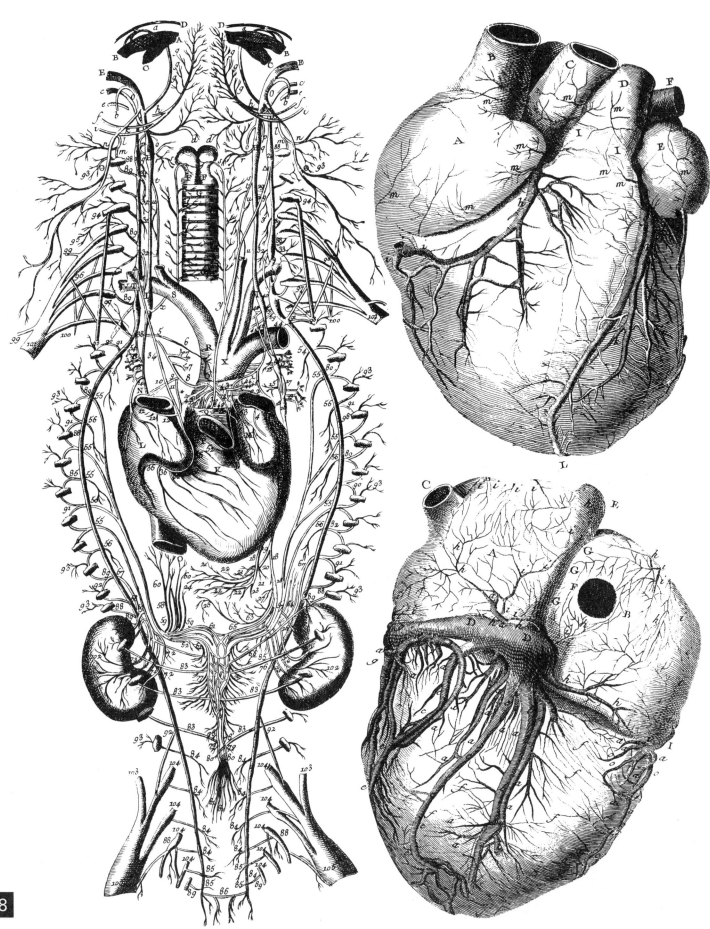

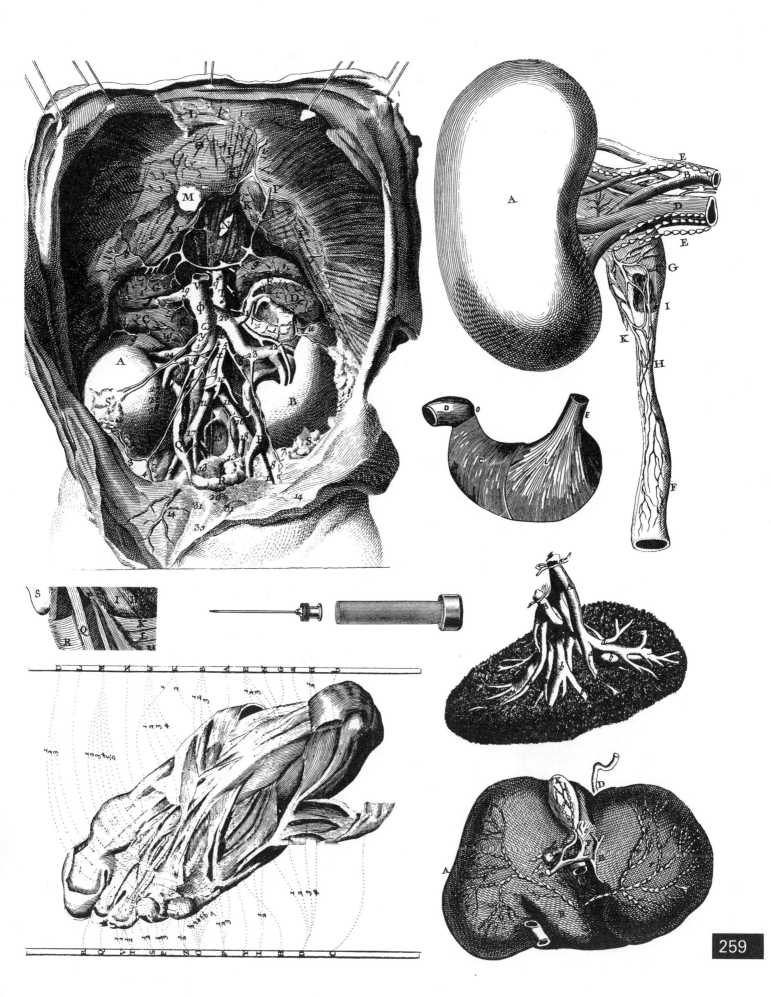

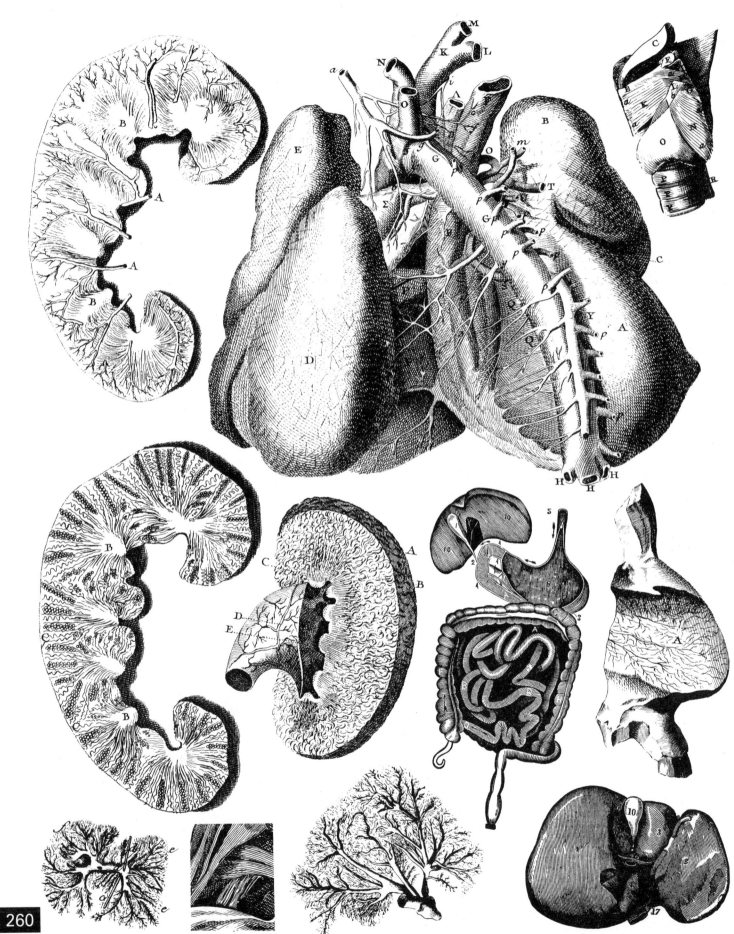

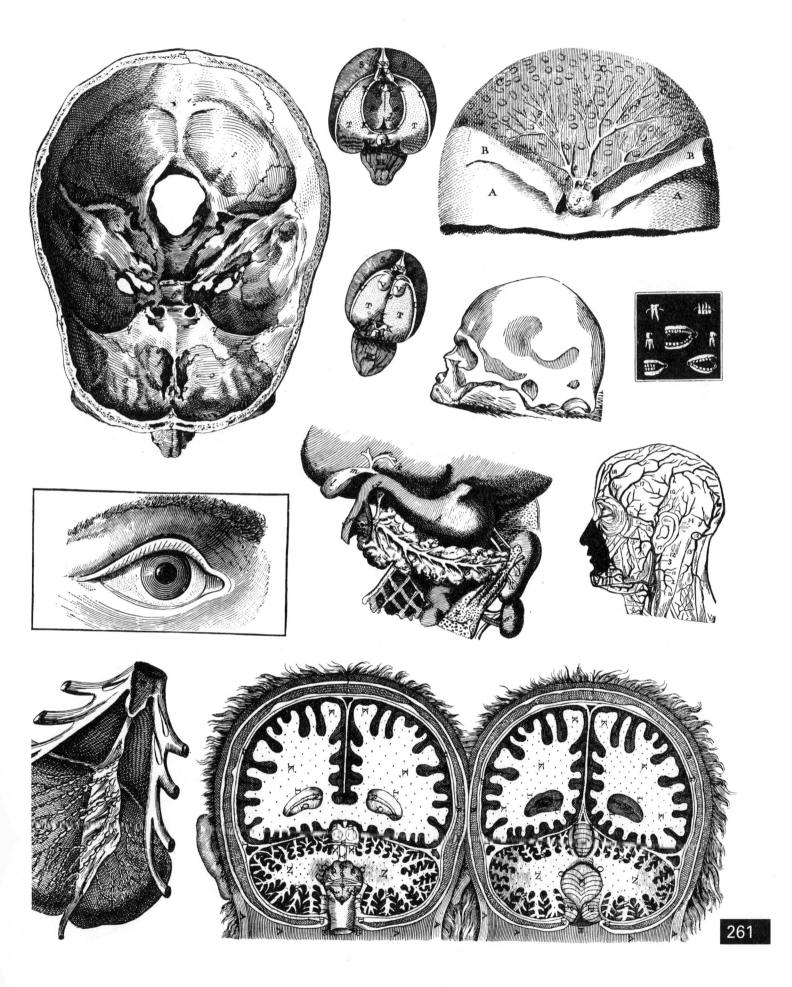

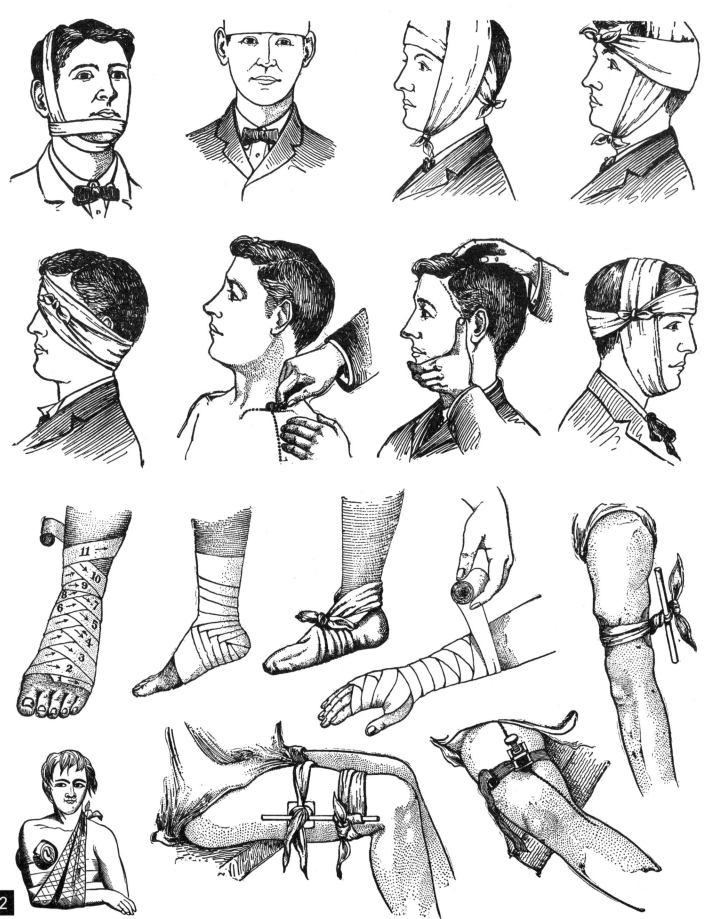

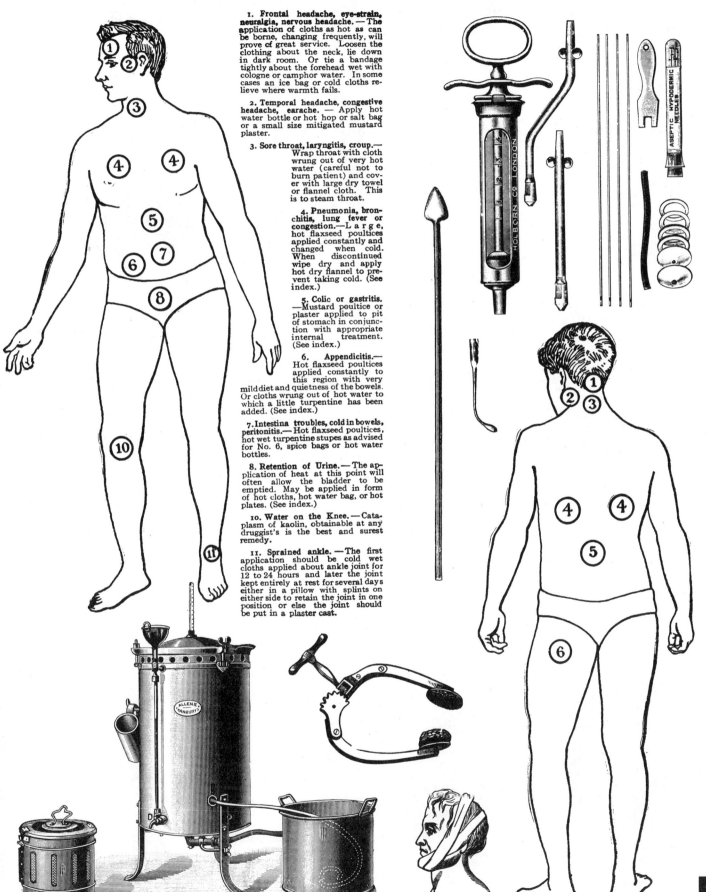

1. **Frontal headache, eye-strain, neuralgia, nervous headache.** — The application of cloths as hot as can be borne, changing frequently, will prove of great service. Loosen the clothing about the neck, lie down in dark room. Or tie a bandage tightly about the forehead wet with cologne or camphor water. In some cases an ice bag or cold cloths relieve where warmth fails.

2. **Temporal headache, congestive headache, earache.** — Apply hot water bottle or hot hop or salt bag or a small size mitigated mustard plaster.

3. **Sore throat, laryngitis, croup.** — Wrap throat with cloth wrung out of very hot water (careful not to burn patient) and cover with large dry towel or flannel cloth. This is to steam throat.

4. **Pneumonia, bronchitis, lung fever or congestion.** — L a r g e, hot flaxseed poultices applied constantly and changed when cold. When discontinued wipe dry and apply hot dry flannel to prevent taking cold. (See index.)

5. **Colic or gastritis.** — Mustard poultice or plaster applied to pit of stomach in conjunction with appropriate internal treatment. (See index.)

6. **Appendicitis.** — Hot flaxseed poultices applied constantly to this region with very mild diet and quietness of the bowels. Or cloths wrung out of hot water to which a little turpentine has been added. (See index.)

7. **Intestinal troubles, cold in bowels, peritonitis.** — Hot flaxseed poultices, hot wet turpentine stupes as advised for No. 6, spice bags or hot water bottles.

8. **Retention of Urine.** — The application of heat at this point will often allow the bladder to be emptied. May be applied in form of hot cloths, hot water bag, or hot plates. (See index.)

10. **Water on the Knee.** — Cataplasm of kaolin, obtainable at any druggist's is the best and surest remedy.

11. **Sprained ankle.** — The first application should be cold wet cloths applied about ankle joint for 12 to 24 hours and later the joint kept entirely at rest for several days either in a pillow with splints on either side to retain the joint in one position or else the joint should be put in a plaster cast.

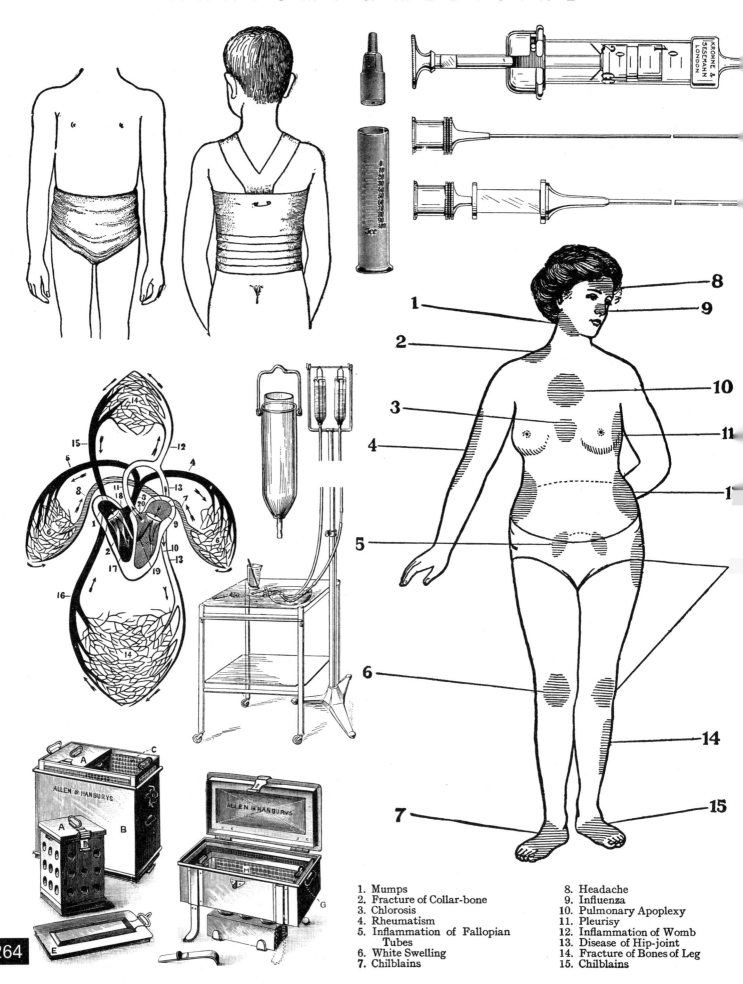

1. Mumps
2. Fracture of Collar-bone
3. Chlorosis
4. Rheumatism
5. Inflammation of Fallopian Tubes
6. White Swelling
7. Chilblains
8. Headache
9. Influenza
10. Pulmonary Apoplexy
11. Pleurisy
12. Inflammation of Womb
13. Disease of Hip-joint
14. Fracture of Bones of Leg
15. Chilblains

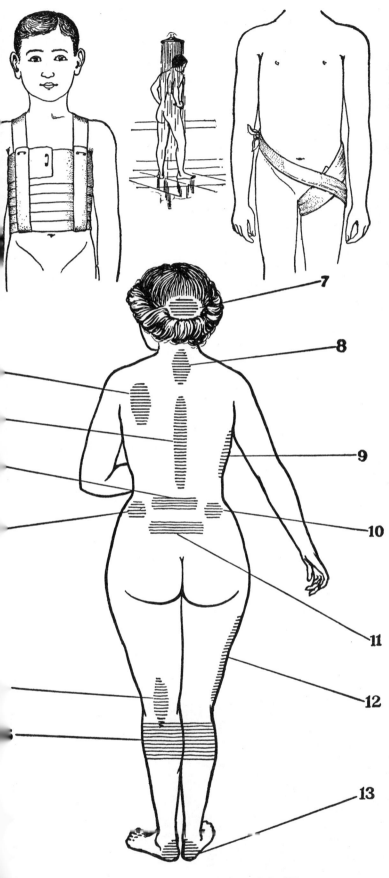

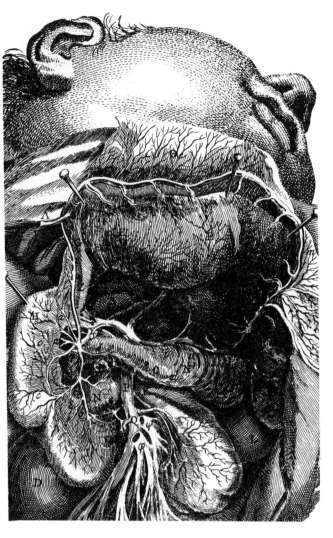

7

8

9

10

11

12

13

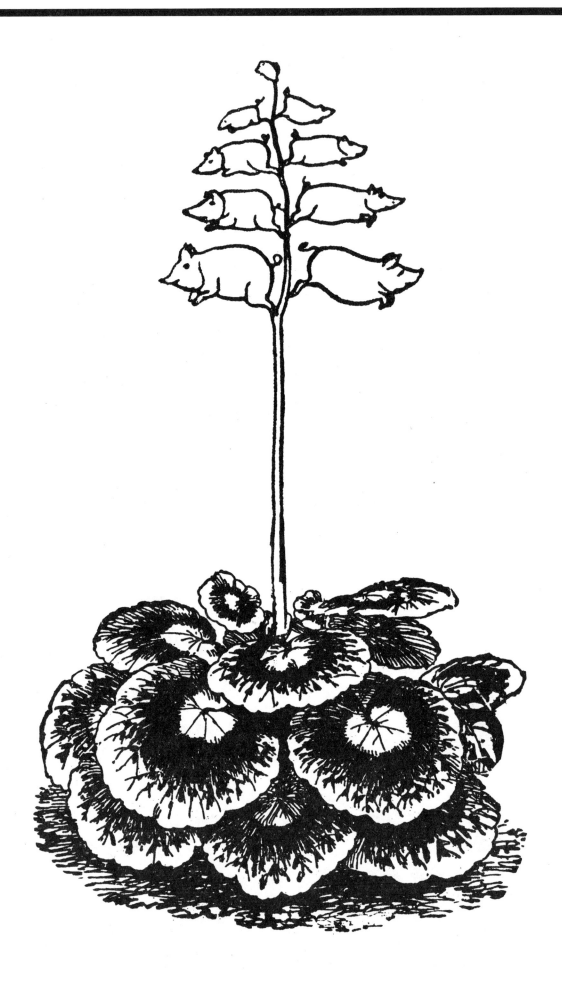

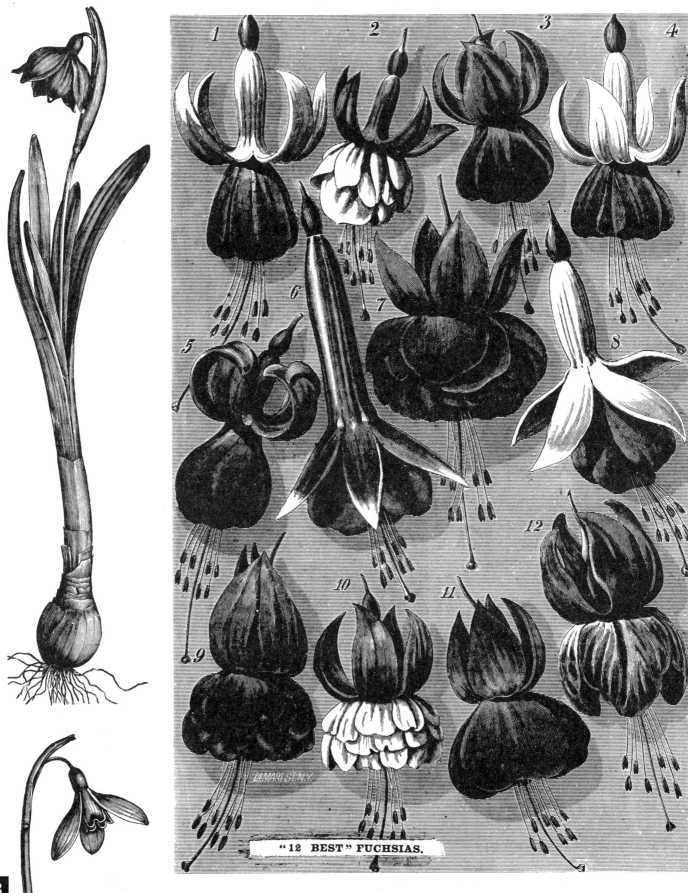

"12 BEST" FUCHSIAS.

FLOWERS

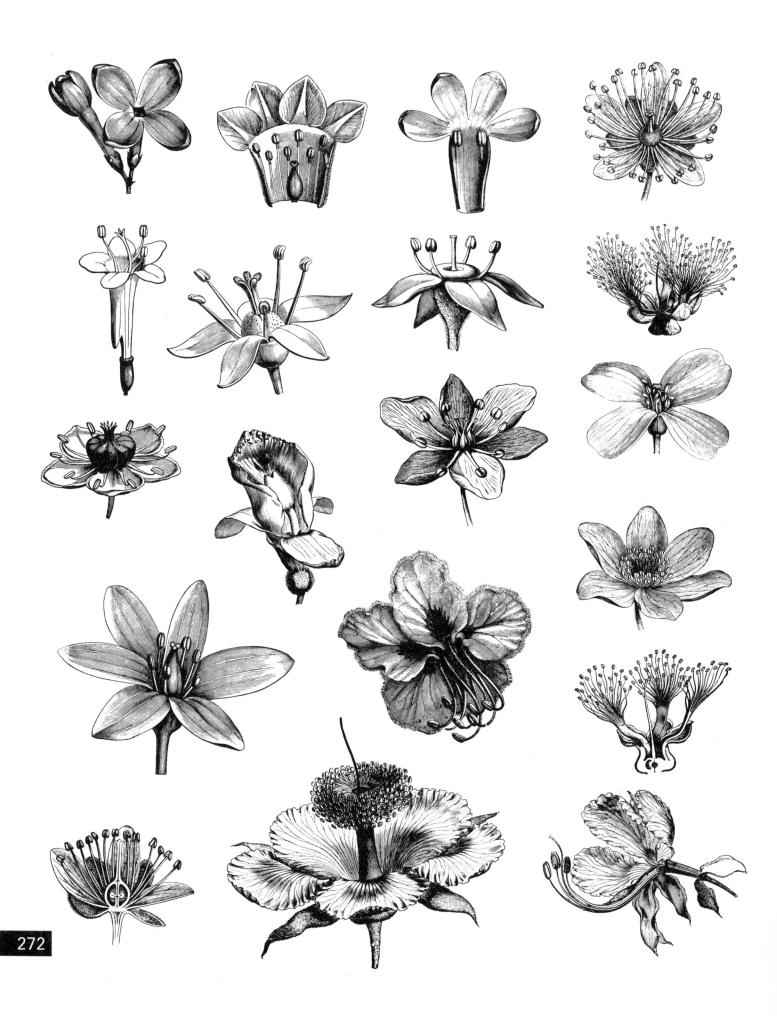

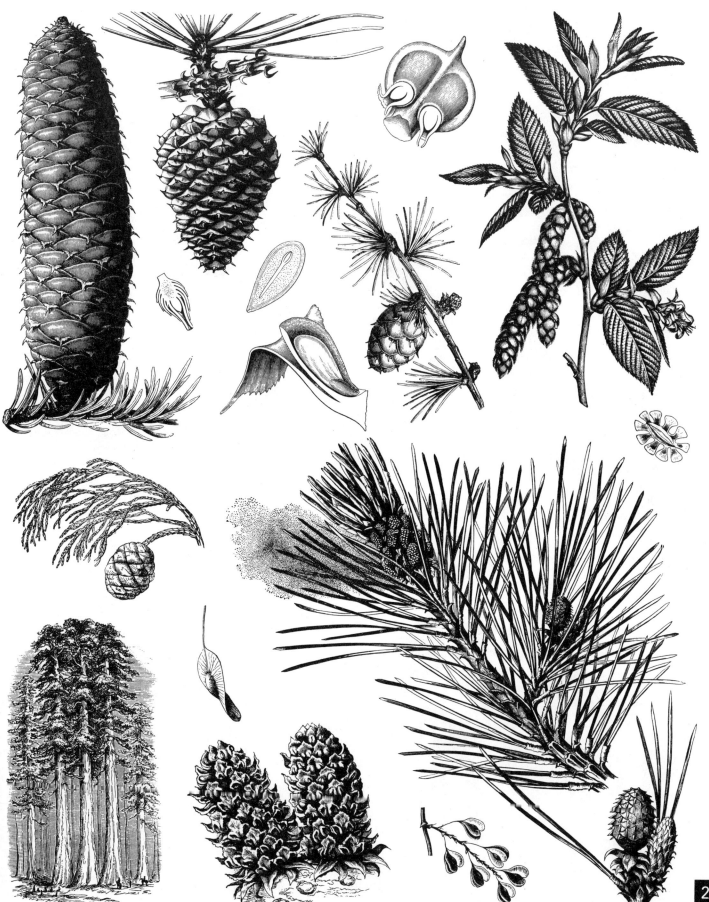

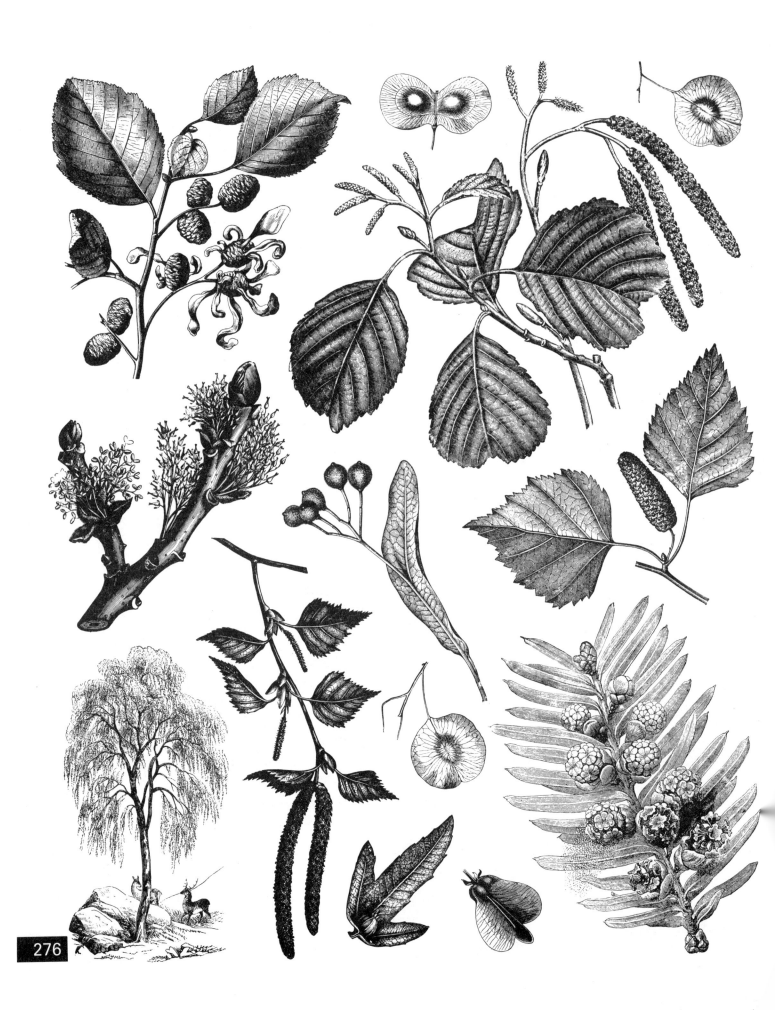

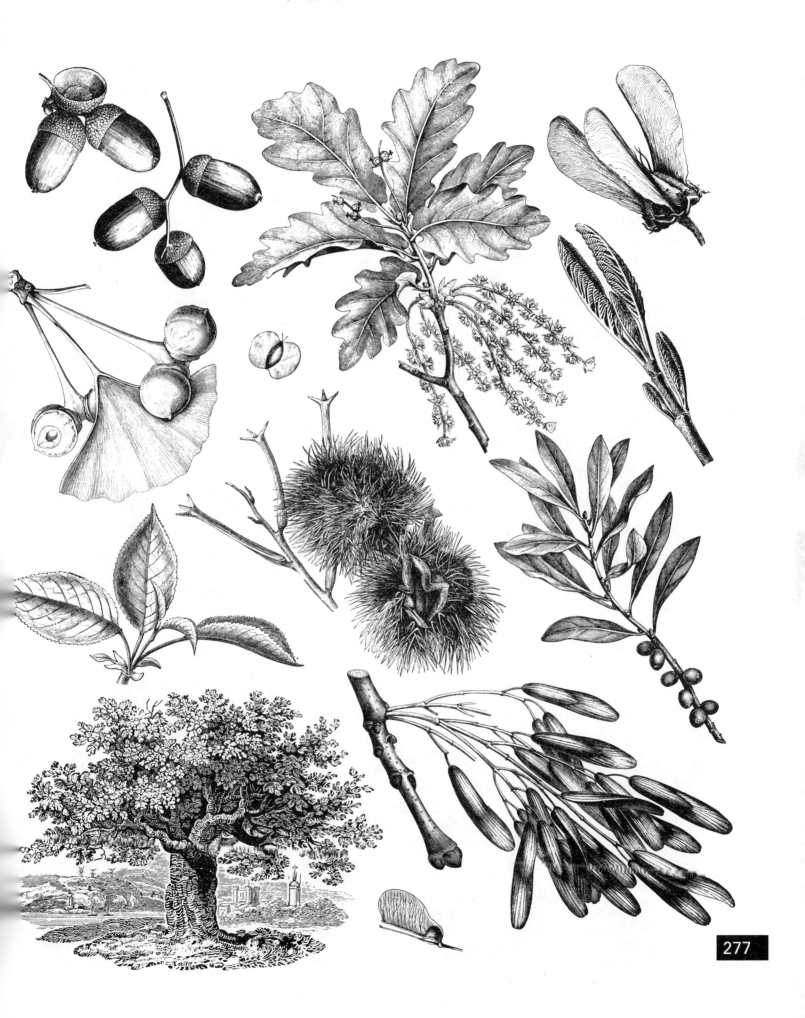

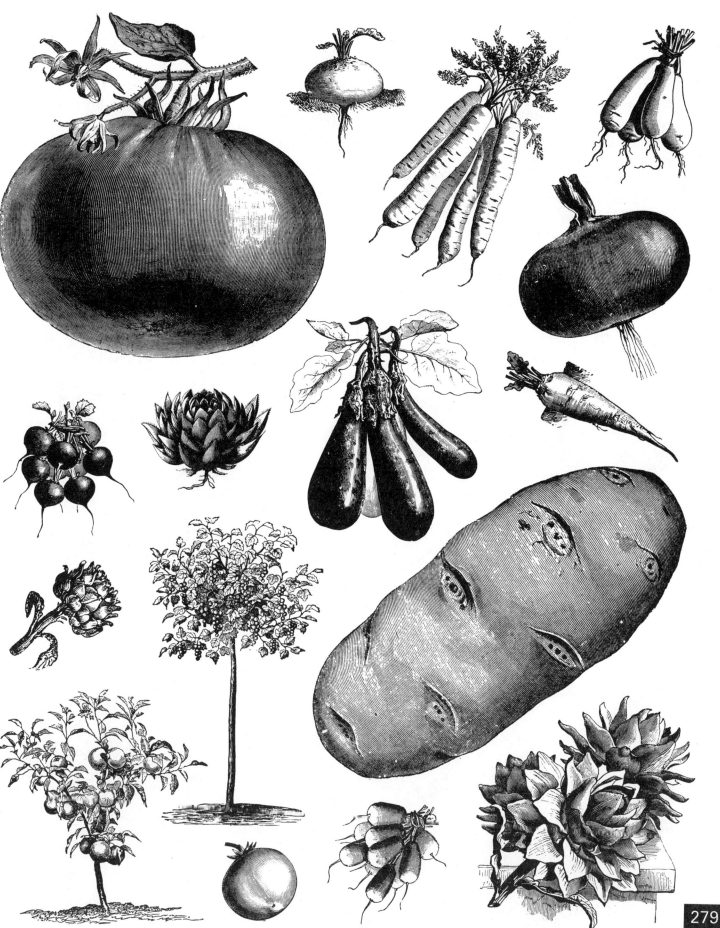

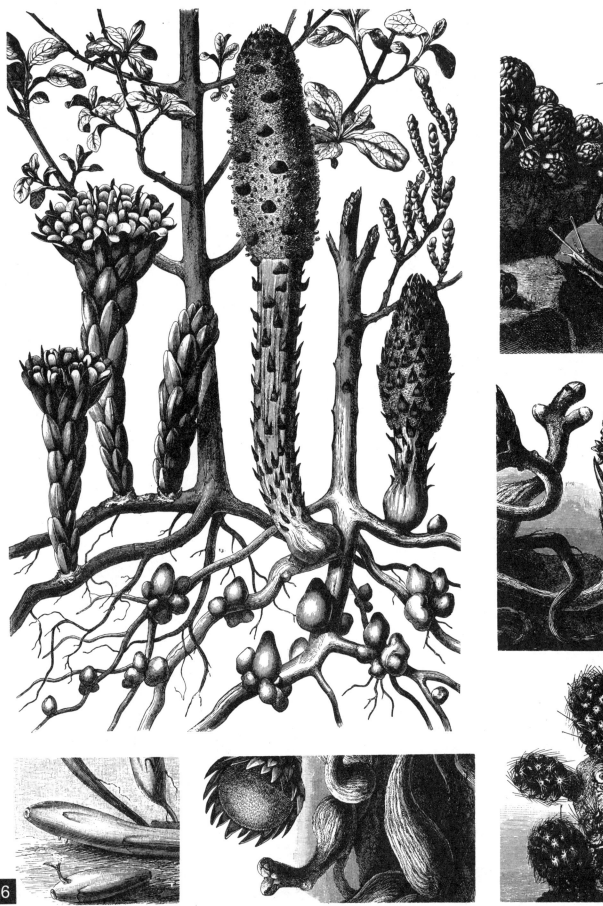

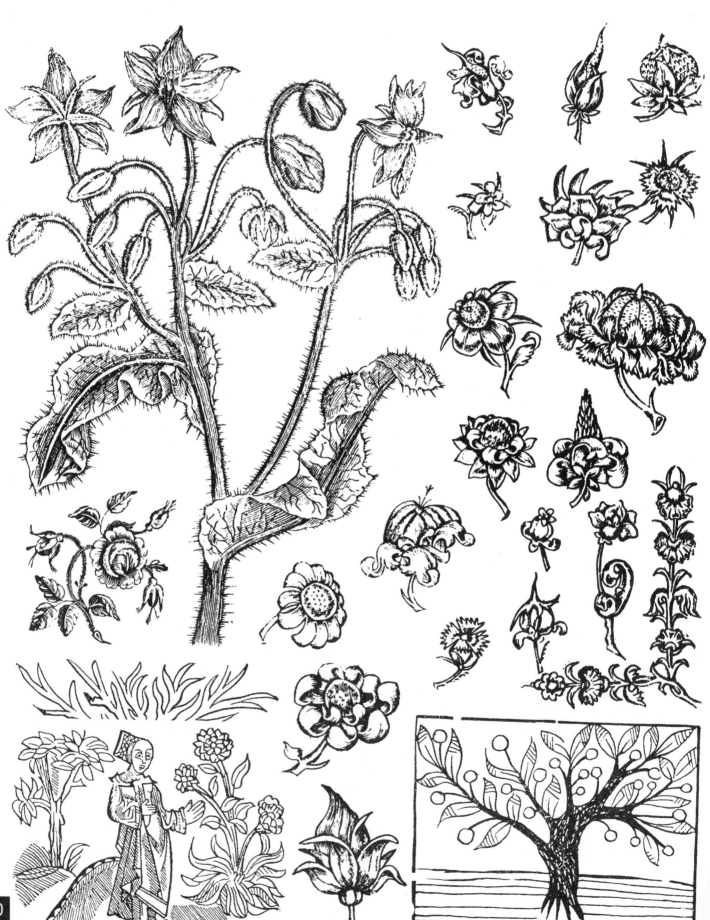

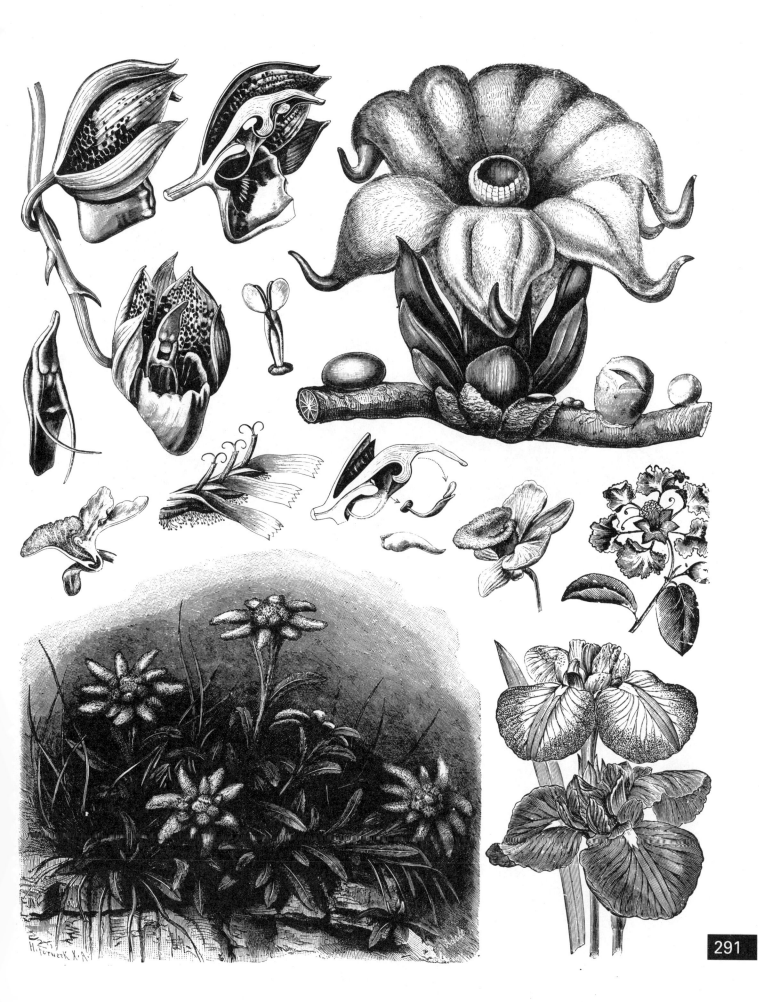

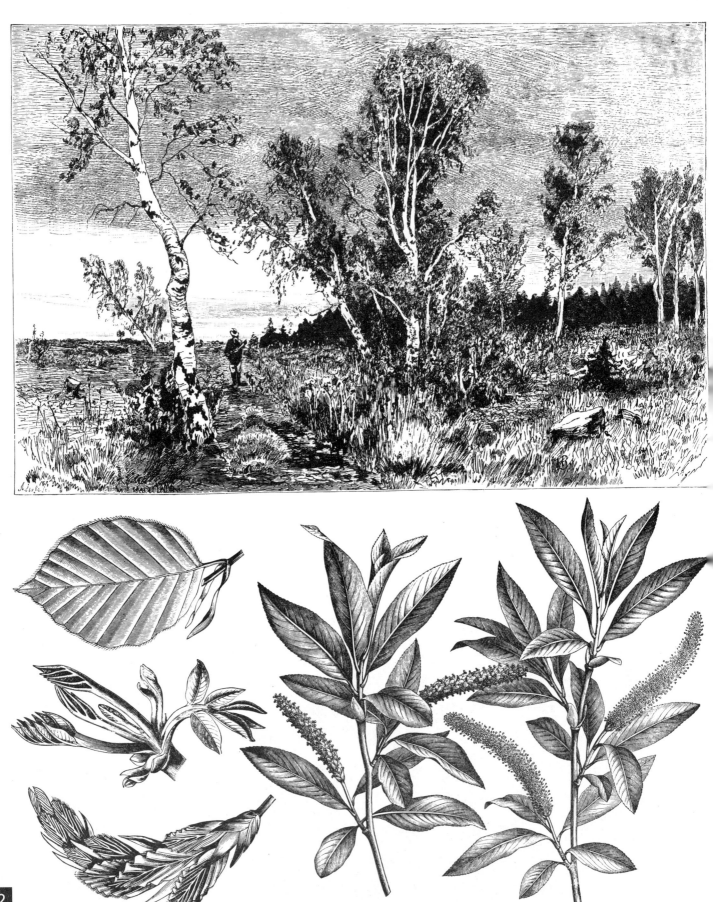

BREVIERE SC.

J. MAISCH · NÜRNBERG

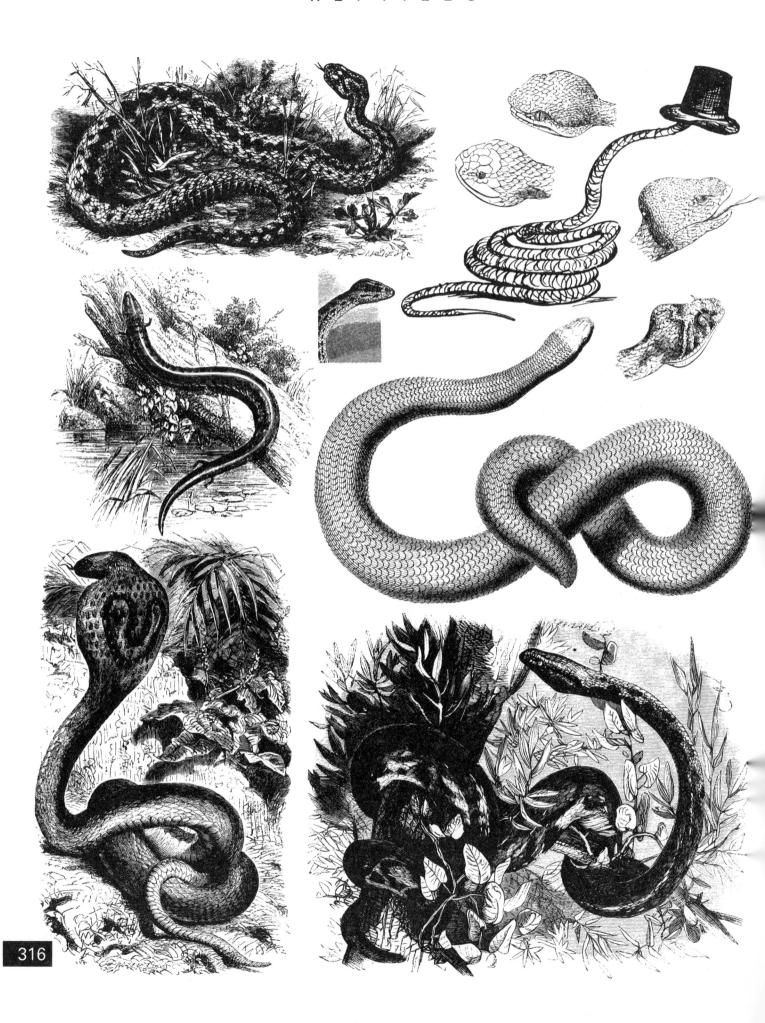

318

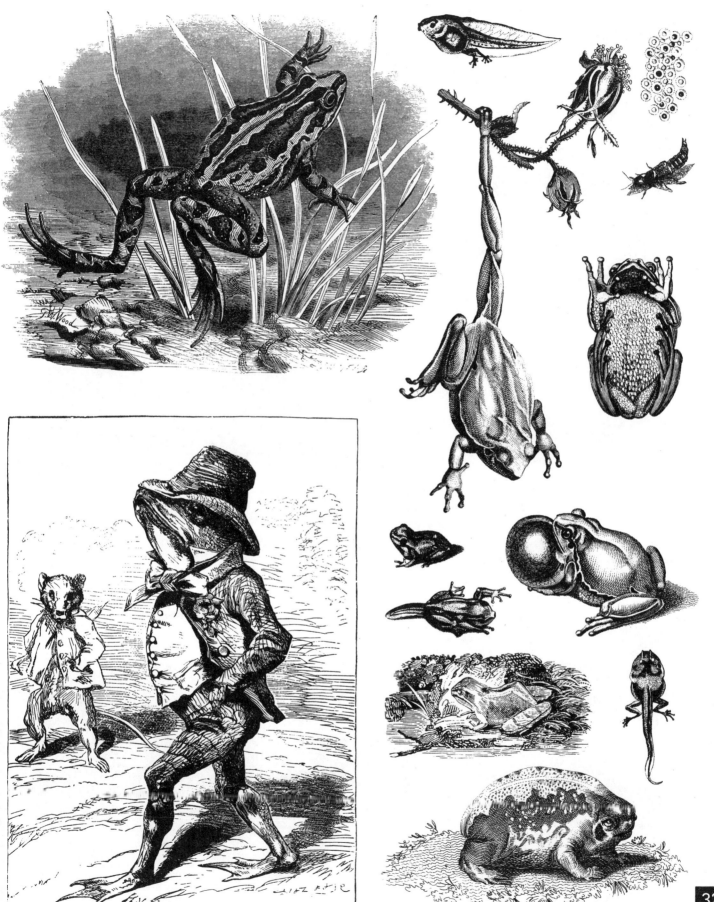

BIRDS

327

BIRDS

329

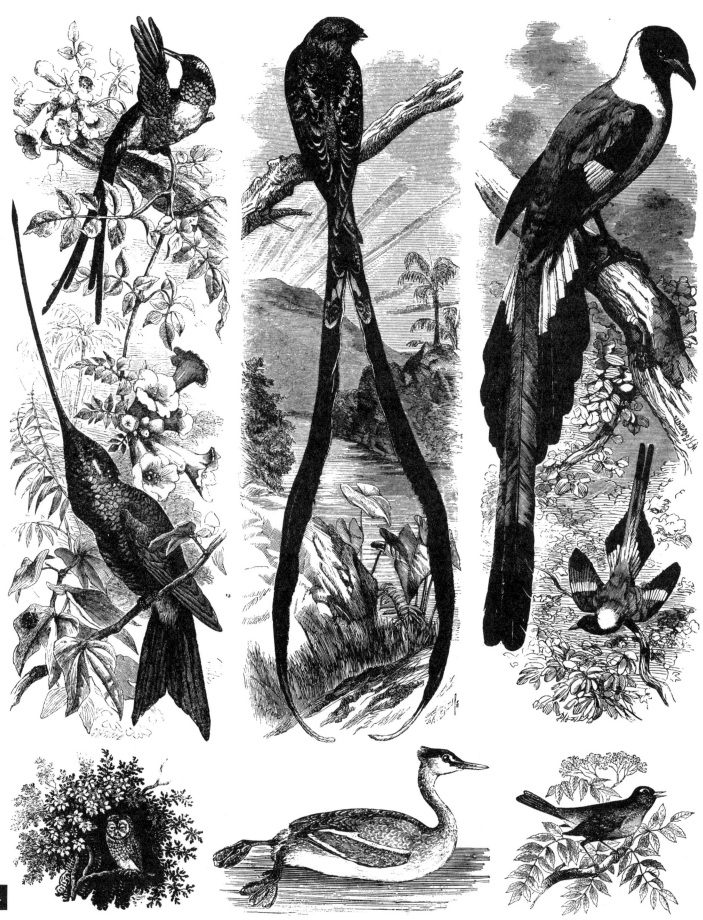

Teal Quail Snipe Plover Ruff

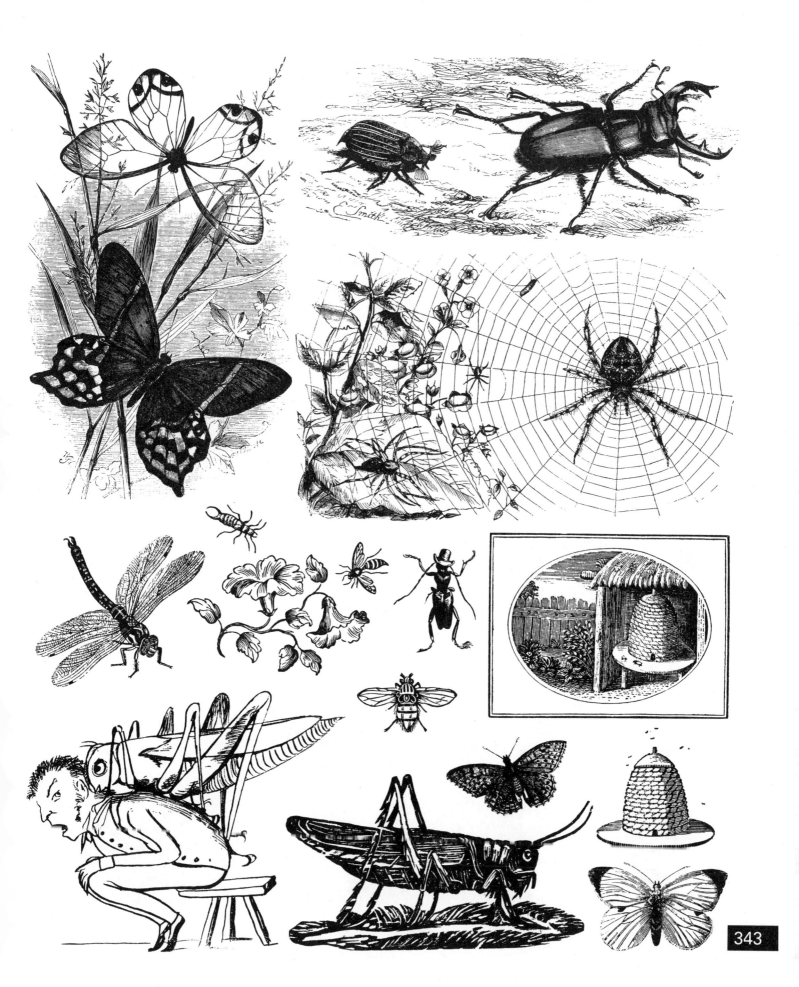

343

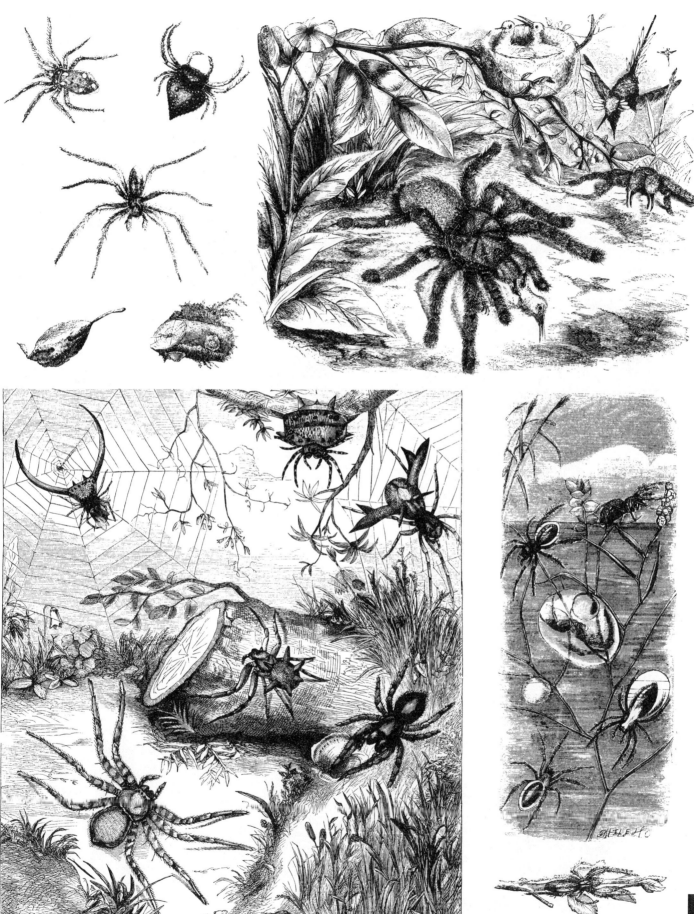

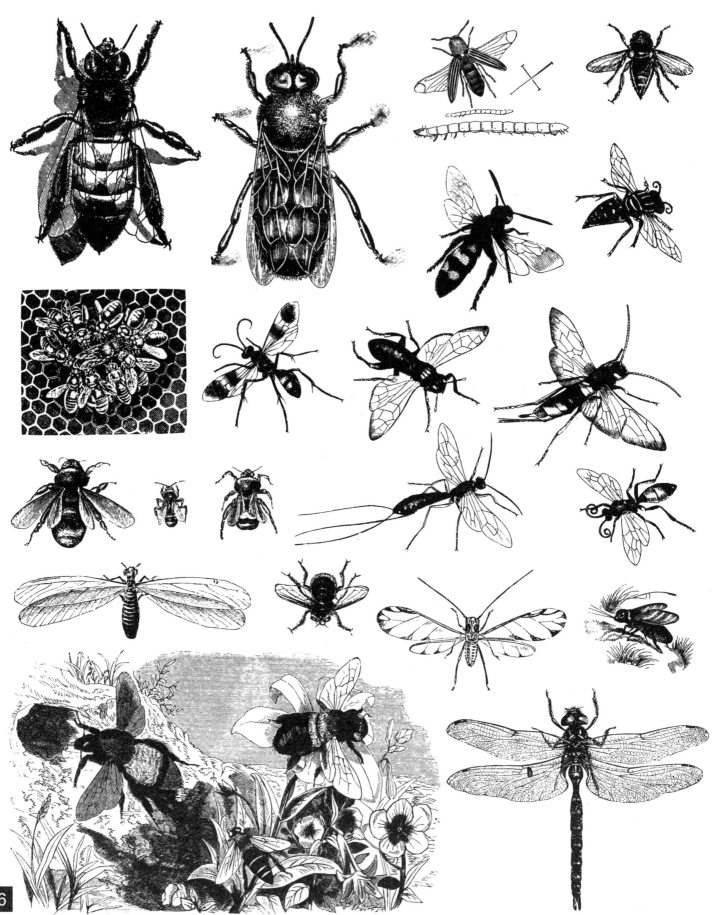

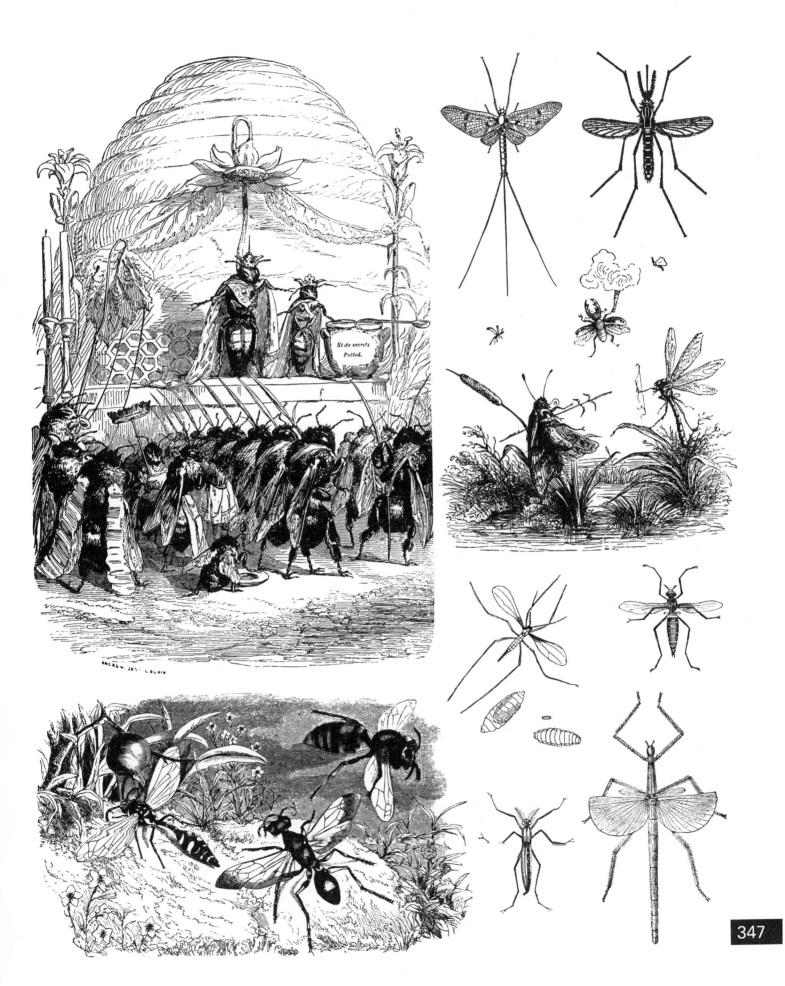

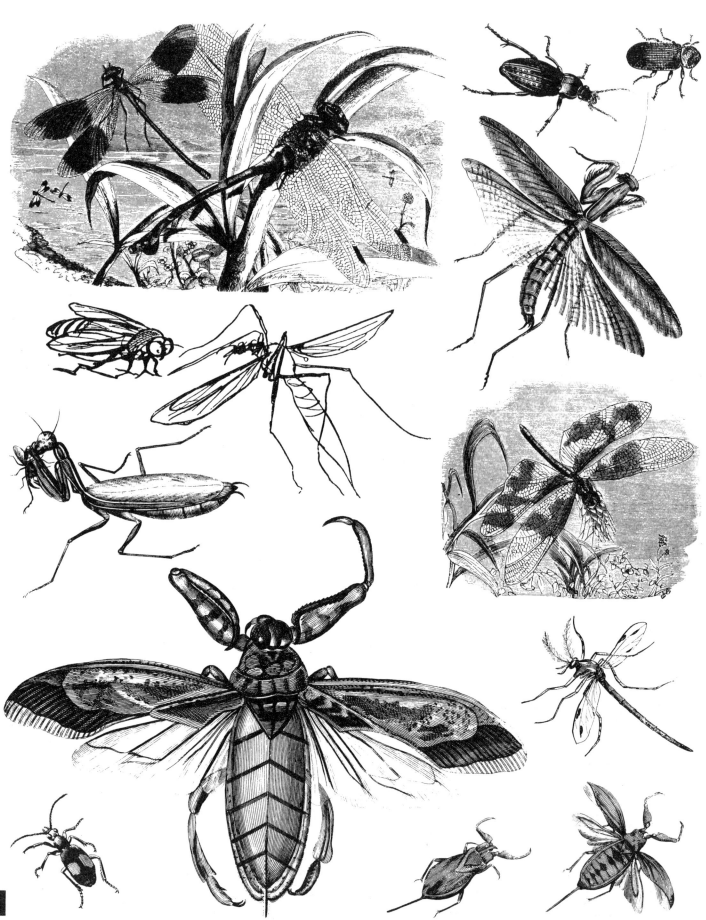

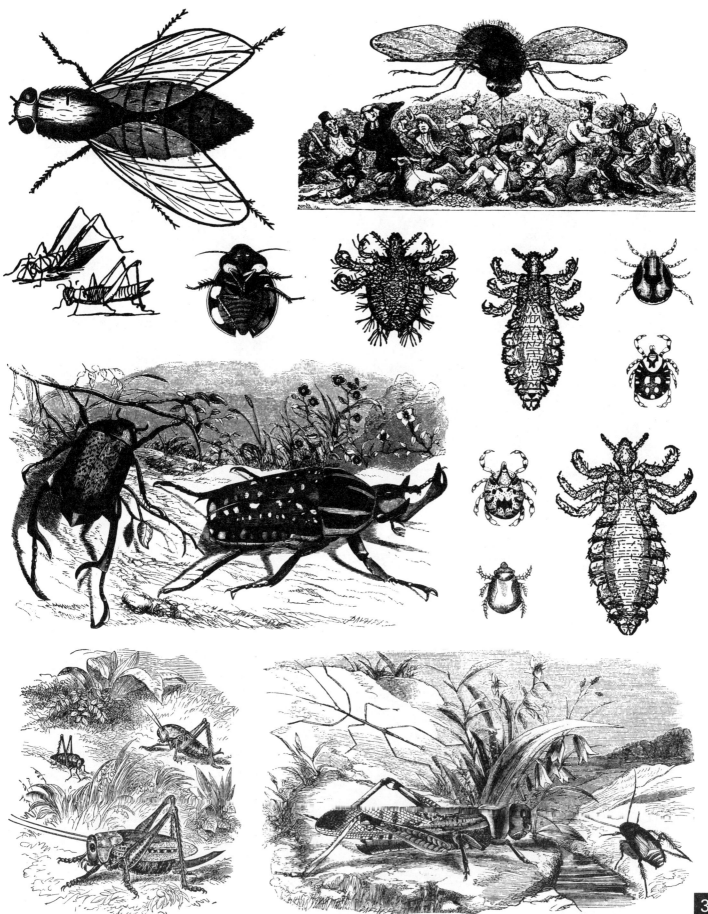

FISH

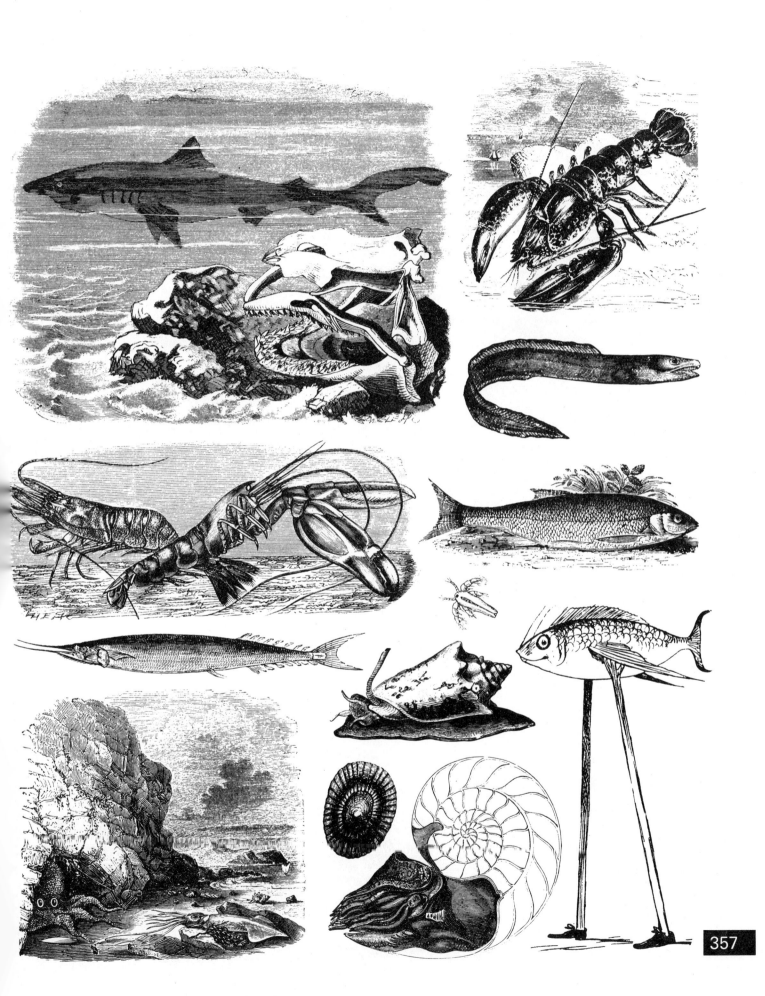

357

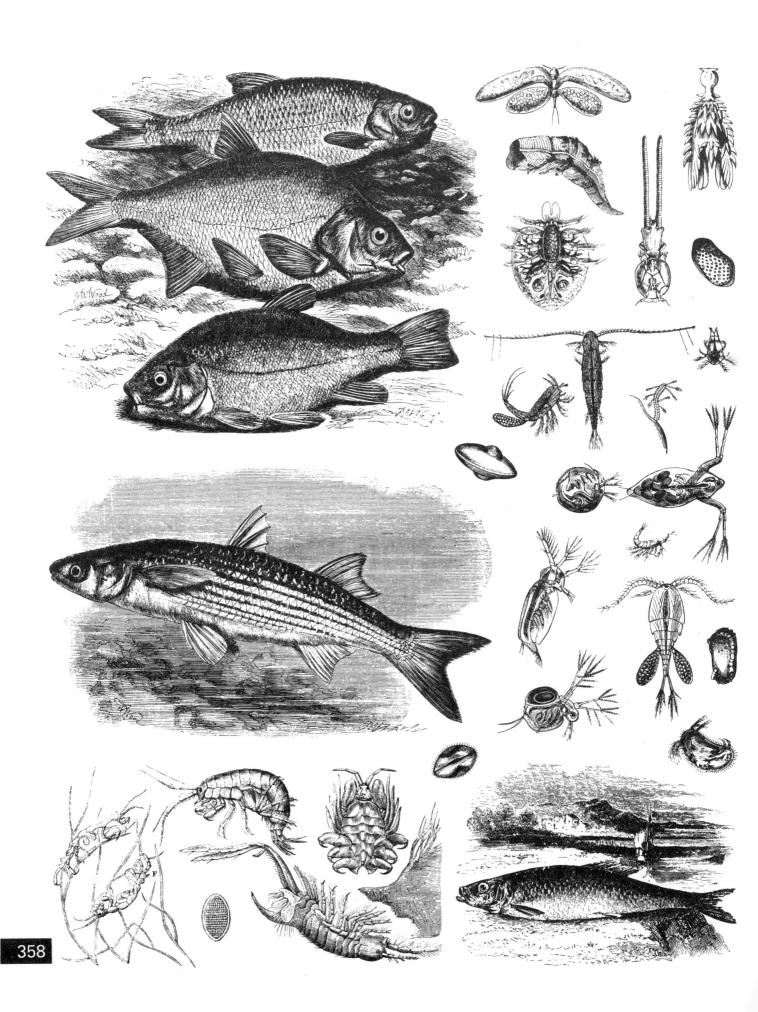

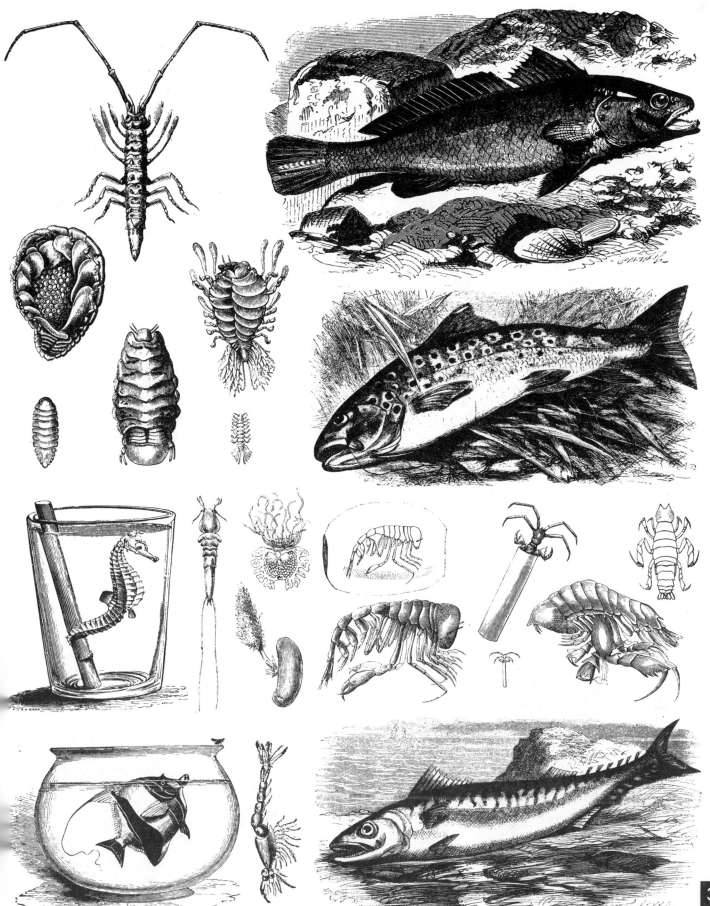

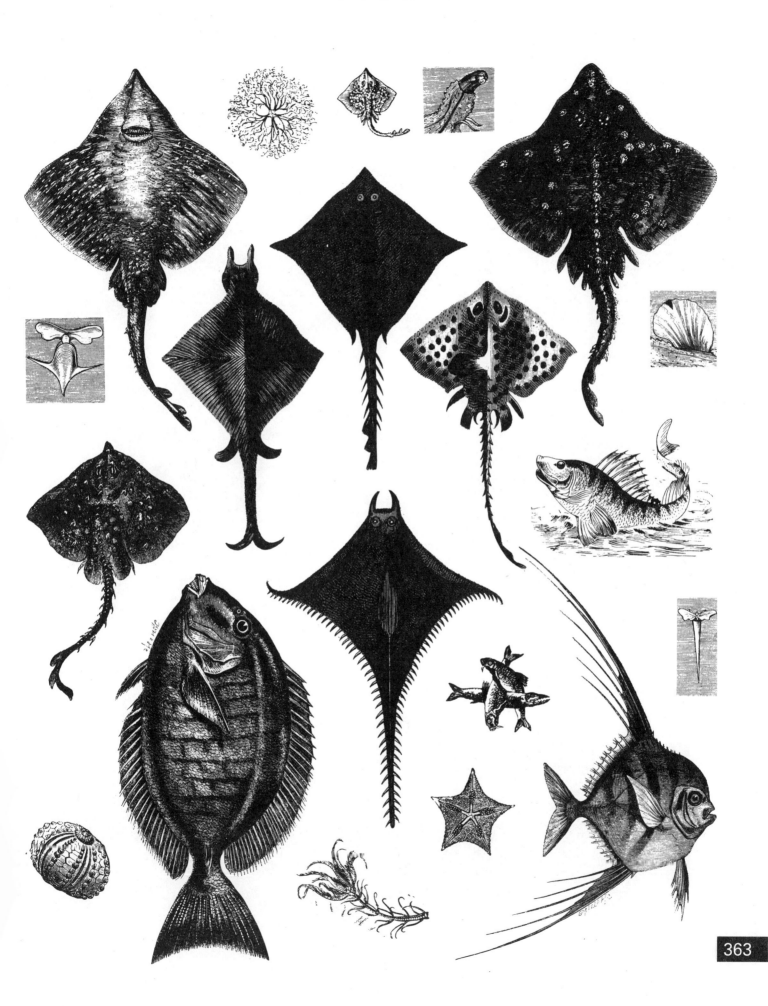

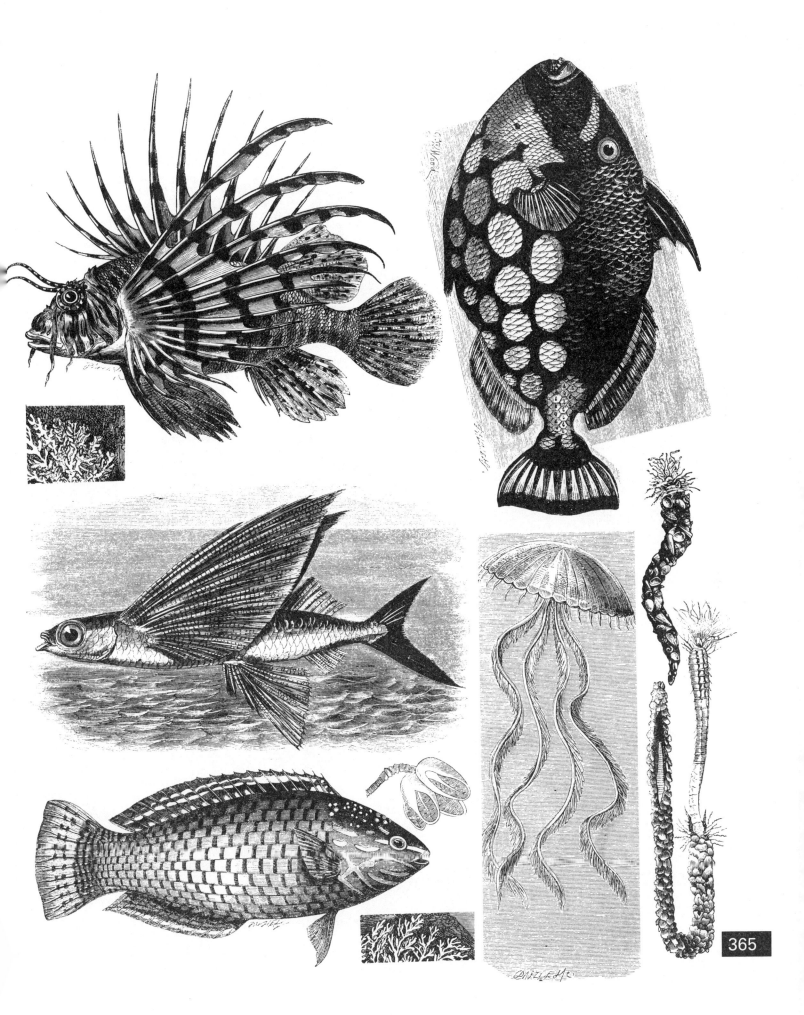

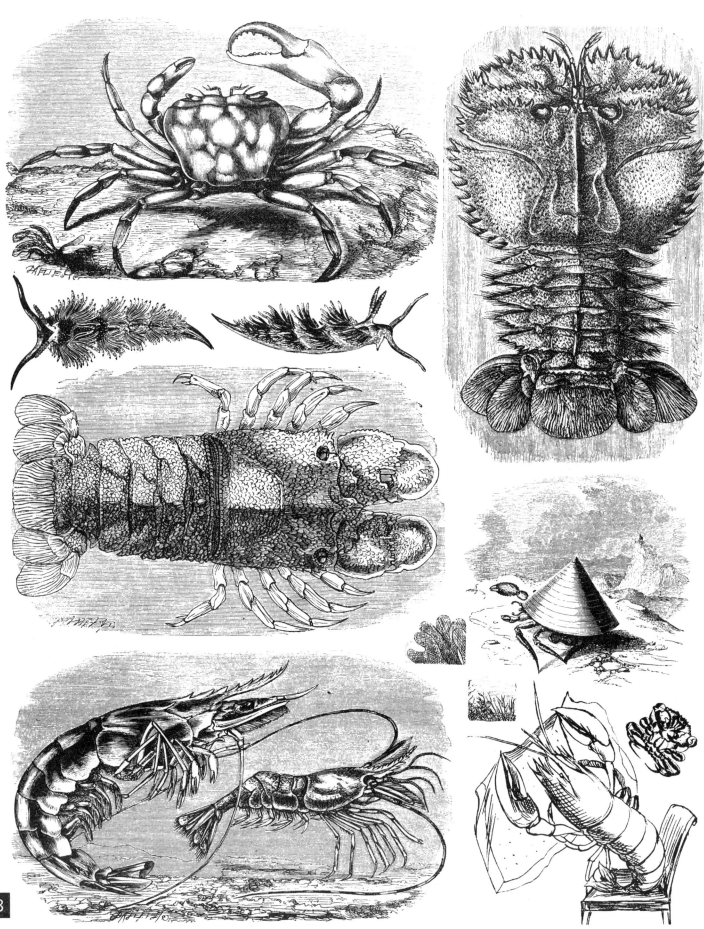

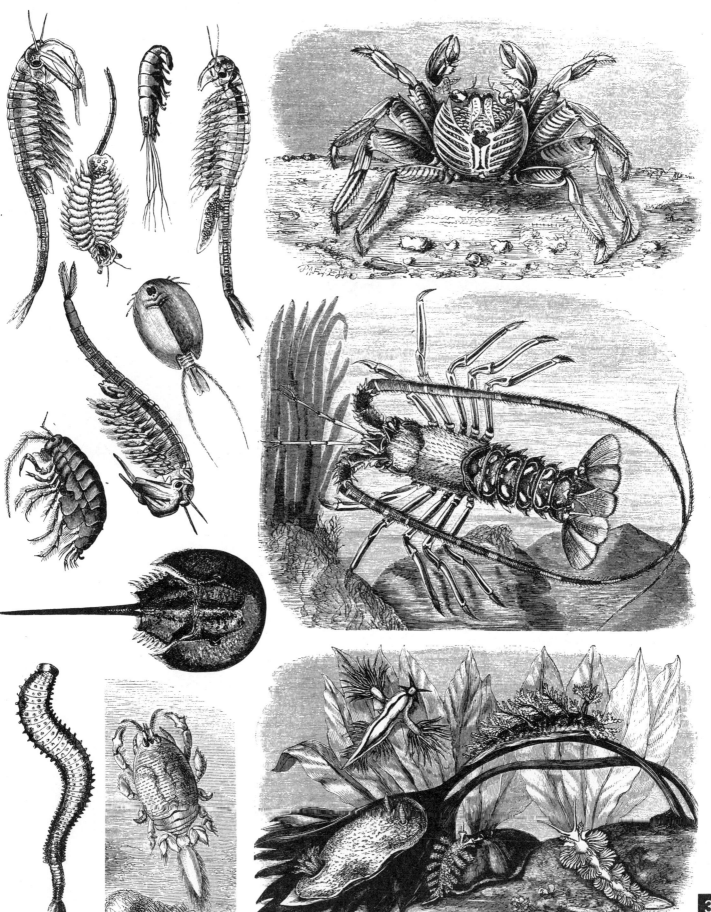

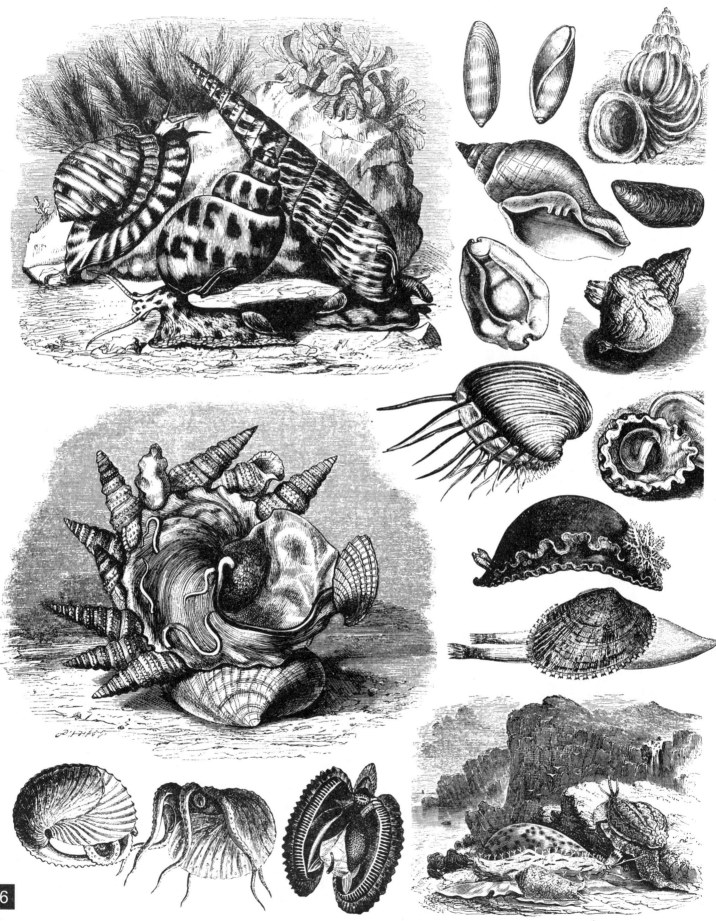

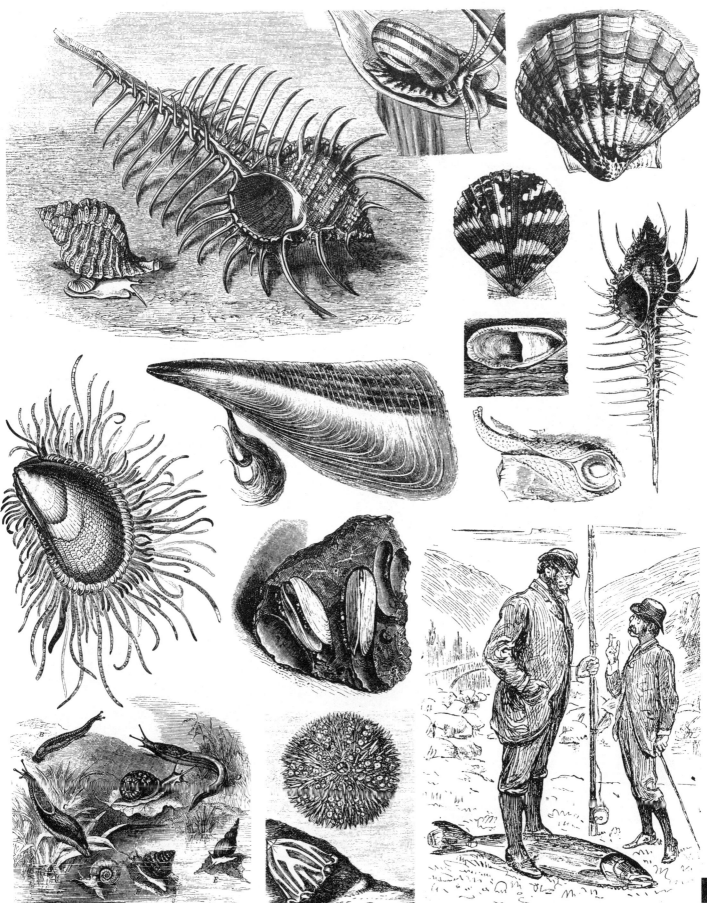

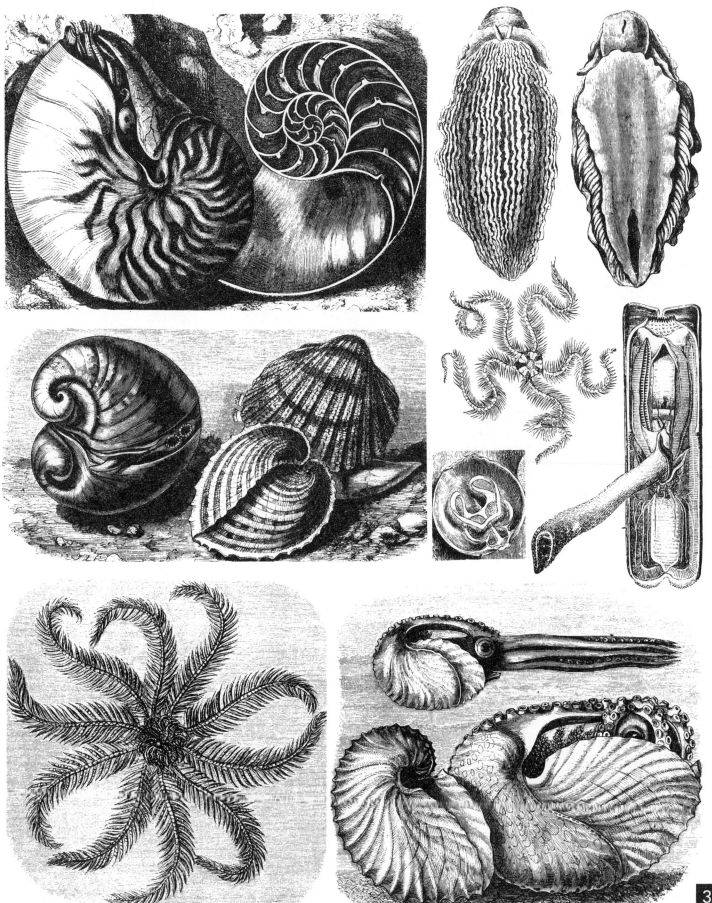

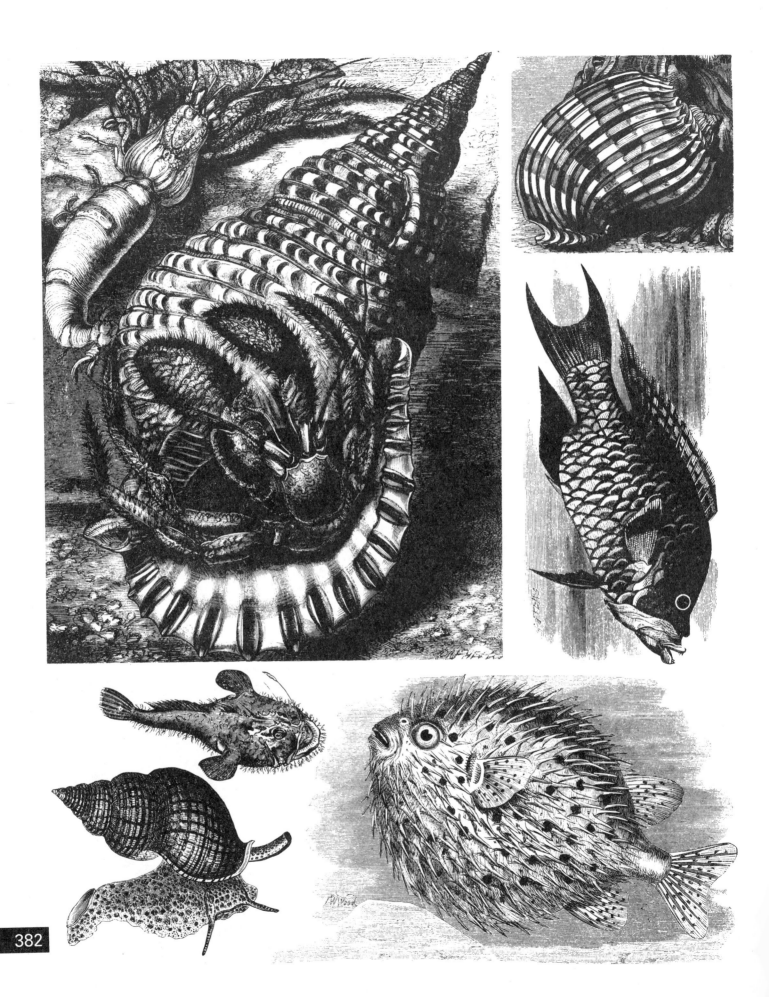